# 100 Frequently Asked Questions About the Special Education Process

W0010541

*This book is dedicated to my wife, Jackie,
and my two children, Jacqueline and Scott,
who provide me with the love and purpose for
undertaking projects that I hope will enhance the lives of
others. My life has been blessed by their loving presence.
I also dedicate this book to my parents, who provided me with
the secure and loving foundation from which to grow; my sister,
Carol, who makes me smile and laugh; and my brother-in-law, George,
who has always been a positive guiding light in my professional journey.*

—R. P.

*This book is dedicated to my wife, Anita,
and two children, Collin and Brittany, who give me the
greatest life imaginable. The long hours and many years
it took to finish this book would never have been possible
without the support of my loving wife. Her constant encouragement,
understanding, and love provide me with the strength I need to
accomplish my goals. I thank her with all my heart. I also dedicate
this book to my parents, who have given me support and guidance
throughout my life. Their words of encouragement and guidance
have made my professional journey a rewarding and successful experience.*

—G. G.

A STEP-BY-STEP GUIDE FOR EDUCATORS

# 100 Frequently Asked Questions About the Special Education Process

ROGER PIERANGELO ~ GEORGE GIULIANI

**CORWIN PRESS**
A SAGE Publications Company
Thousand Oaks, CA 91320

*For information:*

Corwin Press
A Sage Publications Company
2455 Teller Road
Thousand Oaks, California 91320
www.corwinpress.com

Sage Publications Ltd.
1 Oliver's Yard
55 City Road
London, EC1Y 1SP
United Kingdom

Sage Publications India Pvt. Ltd.
B 1/I 1 Mohan Cooperative
    Industrial Area
Mathura Road, New Delhi 110 044
India

Sage Publications Asia-Pacific Pte. Ltd.
33 Pekin Street #02-01
Far East Square
Singapore 048763

Printed in the United States of America

*Library of Congress Cataloging-in-Publication Data*

Pierangelo, Roger.
100 frequently asked questions about the special education process : a step-by-step guide for educators / Roger Pierangelo, George Giuliani.
    p. cm.
Includes bibliographical references and index.
ISBN 978-1-4129-5422-8 (cloth) — ISBN 978-1-4129-1790-2 (pbk.)
    1. Special education—United States. I. Giuliani, George A., 1938- II. Title. III. Title: One hundred frequently asked questions about the special education process.

LC3981.P538 2007
371.9—dc22                                   2006102675

This book is printed on acid-free paper.

07  08  09  10  11  10  9  8  7  6  5  4  3  2  1

| | |
|---|---|
| *Acquisitions Editor:* | Allyson P. Sharp |
| *Editorial Assistant:* | Nadia Kashper |
| *Production Editor:* | Laureen A. Shea |
| *Copy Editor:* | Geoffrey T. Garvey |
| *Typesetter:* | C&M Digitals (P) Ltd. |
| *Proofreader:* | Penny Sippel |
| *Cover Designer:* | Michael Dubowe |

# Contents

# Preface

*100 Frequently Asked Questions About the Special Education Process: A Step-by-Step Guide for Educators* has been developed as an overview and introduction to understanding special education services mandated by federal and state law. There have been many recent changes to the laws guiding special education across the country. It is important to provide information and training for both general and special educators on those changes so that they can be effective teachers when working with exceptional children.

As a professional, you will be working with many professional disciplines in the special education process. You will also need to help parents of children with special needs understand the special education process. Many have no idea about special education and what it really means. As you may be aware, parents and family members are as critical partners as school district personnel in the education of their children. Parents provide essential information to teachers and administrators, play an important role in decisions made about their children, and can be a key to supporting high expectations for their children during their school years (Office of Vocational and Educational Services for Individuals with Disabilities, 2002).

*100 Frequently Asked Questions About the Special Education Process* provides information about laws, regulations, and policies affecting special education programs and services. These protections, rights, and opportunities will best help students reach their full potential when parents, families, and schools work collaboratively. Setting high expectations for students and high standards for programs will provide the greatest opportunities for a successful adult life (Office of Vocational and Educational Services for Individuals with Disabilities, 2002).

*100 Frequently Asked Questions About the Special Education Process* was written to explain the special education process so that, if a child in your class or school does receive special education services, you can work effectively with the administrators, parents, other professionals, and the outside community as a member of the special education team. Special education is meant to meet the unique needs of a child that result from a disability and to ensure that students with disabilities receive all needed aids and services. Special education laws and regulations are meant to protect a student with disabilities and ensure that he or she gets the services and assistance that are necessary to make effective progress. The laws and regulations are also very complex.

*100 Frequently Asked Questions About the Special Education Process* has been developed to answer frequently asked questions about special education. While it is not a complete statement of the procedural safeguards that must be offered, it does describe the key points of state and federal laws affecting the provision of special education and is intended to help give you a working knowledge of the special education process. We hope *100 Frequently Asked Questions About the Special Education Process* will be helpful to you in understanding the key concepts of the law and how to be an effective participant in the special education process as an educator of exceptional children.

## Acknowledgments

In the course of writing this book, we have encountered many professional and outstanding sites. Those resources have contributed and continue to contribute enormous information, support, guidance, and education to parents, students, and professionals in the area of special education. Although we have accessed many worthwhile sites, we especially thank and acknowledge the National Dissemination Center for Children with Disabilities, the Alaska State Department of Education, and the National Institutes of Health.

Dr. Roger Pierangelo and Dr. George Giuliani extend sincere thanks to Allyson Sharp and Laureen Shea at Corwin Press. Their constant encouragement and professionalism made this project a very worthwhile and rewarding experience.

**Roger Pierangelo:** I extend thanks to the following: the faculty, administration, and staff of the Department of Graduate Special Education and Literacy at Long Island University; Ollie Simmons, for her friendship, loyalty, and great personality; the students and parents of the Herricks Public Schools I have worked with and known over the past thirty-five years; the late Bill Smyth, a truly gifted and "extraordinary ordinary" man; and Helen Firestone, for her influence on my career and her tireless support of me.

**George Giuliani:** I extend sincere thanks to all of my colleagues at Hofstra University in the School of Education and Allied Human

Services. I am especially grateful to those who have made my transition to Hofstra University such a smooth one, including Maureen Murphy (dean), Daniel Sciarra (chairperson), Frank Bowe, Diane Schwartz (graduate program director of early childhood special education), Darra Pace, Gloria Wilson, Alan Wenderoff, Laurie Johnson, Joan Bloomgarden, Jamie Mitus, Estelle Gellman, Joseph Lechowicz, Holly Seirup, Adele Piombino, Marjorie Butler, Eve Byrne, and Linda Cappa. I also thank my brother and sister, Roger and Claudia; mother-in-law Ursula Jenkeleit; sisters-in-law Karen and Cindy; and brothers-in-law Robert and Bob. They have provided me with encouragement and reinforcement in all of my personal and professional endeavors.

Corwin Press gratefully acknowledges the contributions of the following reviewers:

Jean Keuker
Retired and now Adjunct Professor
Our Lady of the Lake University
San Antonio, TX

Pamela Tabor
Elementary Math Specialist
Harford County Public Schools
Havre de Grace, MD

Kaycee Taylor
High School Social Studies Teacher
Bainbridge Island High School
Bainbridge Island, WA

Colleen Winkler
Gifted/Talented Education, NBCT
Riverdale High School
Jefferson, LA

Stacy Wright
Explicit Reading Teacher
Lowndes County Schools
Valdosta, GA

# About the Authors

**Roger Pierangelo, PhD,** is an associate professor in the Department of Special Education and Literacy at Long Island University. He has been an administrator of special education programs, served for eighteen years as a permanent member of Committees on Special Education, has over thirty years of experience in the public school system as a general education classroom teacher and school psychologist, and serves as a consultant to numerous private and public schools, PTA, and SEPTA groups. Dr. Pierangelo has also been an evaluator for the New York State Office of Vocational and Rehabilitative Services and a director of a private clinic. He is a New York State–licensed clinical psychologist, a certified school psychologist, and a Board Certified Diplomate Fellow in Student and Adolescent Psychology and Forensic Psychology. Dr. Pierangelo is the executive director of the National Association of Special Education Teachers (NASET) and an executive director of the American Academy of Special Education Professionals (AASEP). He also holds the office of vice president of the National Association of Parents with Children in Special Education (NAPCSE).

Dr. Pierangelo earned his BS from St. John's University, MS from Queens College, Professional Diploma from Queens College, PhD from Yeshiva University, and Diplomate Fellow in Student and Adolescent Psychology and Forensic Psychology from the International College of Professional Psychology. Dr. Pierangelo is a member of the American Psychological Association, New York State Psychological Association, Nassau County Psychological Association, New York State Union of Teachers, and Phi Delta Kappa.

Dr. Pierangelo is the author of multiple books by Corwin Press, including *The Big Book of Special Education Resources* and *The Step-by-Step Series for Special Educators.*

**George Giuliani, JD, PsyD,** is a full-time tenured associate professor and the director of Special Education at Hofstra University's School of Education and Allied Human Services in the Department of Counseling, Research, Special Education, and Rehabilitation. Dr. Giuliani earned his BA from the College of the Holy Cross, MS from St. John's University, JD from City University Law School, and PsyD from Rutgers University, the Graduate School of Applied and Professional Psychology. He earned Board Certification as a Diplomate Fellow in Student and Adolescent Psychology and Forensic Psychology from the International College of Professional Psychology. Dr. Giuliani is also a New York State–licensed psychologist and certified school psychologist and has an extensive private practice focusing on students with special needs. He is a member of the American Psychological Association, New York State Psychological Association, National Association of School Psychologists, Suffolk County Psychological Association, Psi Chi, American Association of University Professors, and the Council for Exceptional Students.

Dr. Giuliani is the president of the National Association of Parents with Children in Special Education (NAPCSE), executive director of the National Association of Special Education Teachers (NASET), and executive director of the American Academy of Special Education Professionals (AASEP). He is a consultant for school districts and early childhood agencies and has provided numerous workshops for parents and guardians and teachers on a variety of special education and psychological topics. Dr. Giuliani is the coauthor of numerous books by Corwin Press, including *The Big Book of Special Education Resources* and *The Step-by-Step Series for Special Educators.*

# Introduction

## Understanding Special Education Jargon

### What Is Special Education?

Under the federal law that protects students in special education and their parents and guardians, the Individuals with Disabilities Education Act (IDEA), special education is defined as *"specially designed instruction, at no cost to the parent/guardians, to meet the unique needs of a student with a disability"* (20 U.S.C.1401(29)).

### In the Definition of Special Education, What Does "Specially Designed Instruction" Mean?

Specially designed instruction means adapting, as appropriate to the needs of a student eligible under the act, the content, methodology, or delivery of instruction

- To address the unique needs of the student that result from the student's disability
- To ensure access of the student to the general curriculum, so that he or she can meet the educational standards within the jurisdiction of the public agency that apply to all students.

### In the Definition of Special Education, What Does "At No Cost to Parents/Guardians" Mean?

At no cost means that all specially designed instruction is provided without charge but does not preclude incidental fees that are normally charged to nondisabled students or their parents or guardians as a part of the general education program.

## In the Definition of Special Education, What Does a "Student With a Disability" Mean?

A student with a disability means *a student evaluated as having mental retardation, a hearing impairment (including deafness), a speech or language impairment, a visual impairment (including blindness), a serious emotional disturbance (referred to in this part as emotional disturbance), an orthopedic impairment, autism, traumatic brain injury, another health impairment, a specific learning disability, deaf-blindness, or multiple disabilities, and who, by reason thereof, needs special education and related services.*

For students ages 3 through 9, a "student with a disability" may include, at the discretion of the state and the local educational agency (LEA), a student who is experiencing *developmental delays,* as defined by the state and as measured by appropriate **diagnostic** instruments and procedures, in one or more of the following areas:

- Physical development
- Cognitive development
- Communication development
- Social or emotional development, *or*
- Adaptive development, *and*
- Who needs, for that reason, special education and **related services**

From birth through age 2, students may be eligible for services through the Infants and Toddlers with Disabilities Program (Part C) of the IDEA.

## Where Is Special Education Instruction Provided?

Special education instruction can be provided in a number of settings, such as in the classroom, in the home, in hospitals and institutions, and in other settings. Public agencies must ensure that a continuum of alternative placements is available to meet the needs of students with disabilities. This continuum must include the placements just mentioned (instruction in general education classes, special classes, special schools, home instruction, and instruction in hospitals and institutions) and make provision for supplementary services (such as **resource room** or **itinerant** instruction) in conjunction with regular class placement. Unless a student's **individualized education program (IEP)** requires some other arrangement, the student must be educated in the school he or she would attend without a disability.

Special education instruction must be provided to students with disabilities in what is known as the **least restrictive environment,** or **LRE**. Both IDEA and its regulations have provisions to ensure that students with disabilities are educated with nondisabled students to the maximum extent appropriate. IDEA's LRE requirements apply to students in public or private institutions or other care facilities. Each state must further ensure that special classes, separate schooling, or other removal of students with disabilities from the general educational environment occur only if the nature or severity of the disability is such that education in regular classes with the use of supplementary aids and services cannot be achieved satisfactorily.

## How Many Students Currently Receive Special Education Services?

According to the U.S. Department of Education (2004), approximately six million school-aged children (ages 6–21) receive special education. The number of students has increased every year since the inception of our original federal special education law, PL 94-142 (today it is known as the Individuals with Disabilities Education Act, PL 108-446). Since 1975, the number of students being provided special education has increased approximately 75 percent.

## What Federal Laws Protect Students With Disabilities?

### Education for All Handicapped Students Act (EHA)

The passage of Public Law 94-142, Education for All Handicapped Students Act (EHA) by Congress in November 1975 was the end result of many years of litigation and state legislation to protect and promote the civil rights of all students with disabilities. This federal law required states to provide "a free, appropriate public education for every student between the ages of 3 and 21 (unless state law does not provide free, public education to students 3 to 5 or 18 to 21 years of age) regardless of how, or how seriously, he may be handicapped." PL 94-142 was the first law to clearly define the rights of disabled students to free appropriate public education. PL 94-142

- Was the first law to clearly define the rights of disabled students to **free appropriate public education (FAPE)**
- Required the school systems to include the parents and guardians when meeting about the student or making decisions about his or her education
- Mandated an individualized education program (IEP) for every student with a disability (The IEP must include short- and long-term goals for the student, as well as ensure that the necessary services and products are available to the student.)
- Required that students be placed in the least restrictive environment (LRE; LRE means placing the student in the most normal setting that is possible.)
- Ensured that students with disabilities be given nondiscriminatory tests (tests that take into consideration the **native language** of the student and the effects of the disability)
- Required **due process** procedures to be in place (to protect families and students)

## Education of the Handicapped Act Amendments

In 1986, EHA was amended by PL 99-457, the Education of the Handicapped Act Amendments. These amendments, which are also known as the Early Intervention Amendments to PL 94-142, extended FAPE to all students ages 3 to 5 by October 1991 (Section 619, Part B) in all states that wanted to participate (all 50 wanted to and did, even states that do not have public schooling for students at those ages). In Section 619, Part H, a new program was created for infants, toddlers, and their families, which required the development of an individualized family service plan (IFSP) for each student in each family served.

Provisions were also included to help states develop early **intervention** programs for infants and toddlers with disabilities; this part of the legislation became known as the Part H Program. In 1997, the amendments to IDEA were amended and the section of the law that applies to infants and toddlers changed to Part C.

## Individuals with Disabilities Education Act

The EHA was amended again in 1990 by PL 101-476, which, among other things, changed the name of the legislation to the Individuals with Disabilities Education Act, or IDEA. More important,

PL 101-476 replaced the word *handicapped* with the word *disabled* and thereby expanded the services for the affected students. IDEA reaffirms PL 94-142's requirements of a free appropriate public education through an individualized education program with related services and due process procedures. This act also supports the amendments to PL 94-142 that expanded the entitlement in all states to ages 3 to 21, designated assistive technology as a related service in IEPs, strengthened the law's commitment to greater **inclusion** in community schools (least restrictive placement), provided funding for infant and toddler early intervention programs, and required that by age 16 every student have explicitly written in the IEP a plan for transition to employment or postsecondary education.

## Individuals with Disabilities Education Act Amendments of 1997

The IDEA was first amended in 1992 by PL 102-119. The newest amendments to this law were the Individuals with Disabilities Education Act Amendments of 1997 (PL 105-17). These amendments restructured IDEA into four parts: Part A addressed general provisions; Part B covered assistance for education of all students with disabilities; Part C covered infants and toddlers with disabilities; and Part D addressed national activities to improve the education of students with disabilities.

## Individuals with Disabilities Education Improvement Act of 2004

On December 3, 2004, the Individuals with Disabilities Education Improvement Act of 2004 was enacted into law as Public Law 108-446. The statute, as passed by Congress and signed by President George W. Bush, reauthorized and made significant changes to the Individuals with Disabilities Education Act.

The Individuals with Disabilities Education Act, as amended by the Individuals with Disabilities Education Improvement Act of 2004, is intended to help students with disabilities to achieve high standards—by promoting accountability for results, enhancing parent and guardian involvement, and using proven practices and materials—and also by providing more flexibility and reducing paperwork burdens for teachers, states, and local school districts.

Enactment of the new law provides an opportunity to consider improvements in the current regulations that would strengthen the federal effort to ensure that every student with a disability have available a free appropriate public education that (1) is of high quality and (2) is designed to achieve the high standards reflected in the

Elementary and Secondary Education Act of 1965, as amended by the No Child Left Behind Act of 2001 (NCLB) and its implementing regulations.

## Section 504 of the Rehabilitation Act of 1973

A student with a disability who does not need special education but who needs a related service may be eligible for that service under a federal law, **Section 504** of the Rehabilitation Act of 1973.

Section 504 covers qualified students with disabilities who attend schools receiving federal financial assistance. To be protected under Section 504, a student must be determined to (1) have a physical or mental impairment that substantially limits one or more major life activities, (2) have a record of such an impairment, or (3) be regarded as having such an impairment. Section 504 requires that school districts provide a free and appropriate public education to qualified students in their jurisdictions who have a physical or mental impairment that substantially limits one or more major life activities.

To determine whether a student is protected by Section 504, an evaluation would need to be conducted to determine whether he or she is a person with disabilities within the meaning of Section 504. Public elementary and secondary school districts receiving federal financial assistance are required by Section 504 to provide a free appropriate public education to students with disabilities in their jurisdiction.

Decisions about what educational and related services are appropriate for a student under Section 504 must be made by a placement group including persons knowledgeable about the student, the meaning of evaluation data, and placement options. The placement group decides whether the student needs regular or special education and related aids and services. Section 504 also applies to recipients of federal financial assistance that operate private elementary and secondary education programs. These recipients may not, on the basis of handicap, exclude a qualified handicapped person from such programs if the person can, with minor adjustments, be provided an appropriate education within the recipient's program.

The determination of whether a student has a physical or mental impairment that substantially limits a major life activity must be made on the basis of an individual inquiry. Section 504 regulation defines a physical or mental impairment as *any physiological disorder or condition, cosmetic disfigurement, or anatomical loss affecting one or more of the following body systems: neurological; musculoskeletal; special sense organs; respiratory, including speech organs; cardiovascular; reproductive;*

*digestive; genito-urinary; hemic and lymphatic; skin; and endocrine; or any mental or psychological disorder, such as mental retardation, organic brain syndrome, emotional or mental illness, and specific learning disabilities.* The regulation does not set forth an exhaustive list of specific diseases and conditions that may constitute physical or mental impairments because of the difficulty of ensuring the comprehensiveness of such a list.

Major life activities include functions such as caring for one's self, performing manual tasks, walking, seeing, hearing, speaking, breathing, learning, and working. This list is not exhaustive. Other functions can be major life activities for the purposes of Section 504.

## What Is the Purpose of the Individuals with Disabilities Education Act (IDEA)?

IDEA states four specific purposes of the act:

1. To ensure that all students with disabilities have available to them a free appropriate public education that emphasizes special education and related services designed to meet their unique needs and prepare them for further education, employment, and independent living

2. To ensure that the rights of students with disabilities and their parents or guardians are protected

3. To assist states, localities, educational service agencies, and federal agencies to provide for the education of all students with disabilities

4. To assess and ensure the effectiveness of efforts to educate students with disabilities

## What Is a Free Appropriate Public Education?

Under IDEA, a free appropriate public education (FAPE) means special education and related services that

- Are provided to students and youth with disabilities at public expense, under public supervision and direction, and without charge

- Meet the standards of the state education agency (SEA), including the requirements of the IDEA
- Include preschool, elementary school, or secondary school education in the state
- Are provided in keeping with an individualized education program (IEP) that meets the requirements of law

## Who Is Considered a Parent or Guardian Under IDEA?

A parent or guardian of a student with a disability can include

- A natural or adoptive parent or guardian of a student
- A foster parent or guardian, unless state law, regulations, or contractual obligations with a state or local entity prohibit a foster parent or guardian from acting as a parent or guardian
- A guardian (but not the state if the student is a ward of the state)
- An individual acting in the place of a natural or adoptive parent or guardian (including a grandparent-guardian, stepparent-guardian, or other relative) with whom the student lives, or an individual who is legally responsible for the student's welfare
- A **surrogate parent** or guardian who has been appointed in accordance with IDEA regulations, sometimes referred to as an educational surrogate parent (ESP; an ESP is a trained volunteer who is appointed as an **advocate** for a student who is in state custody, such as foster care, and whose parent or guardians are unable or unwilling to advocate for that student)

Also note that if a judicial decree or order identifies a specific person or persons to act as the parent or guardian of a student or to make educational decisions on behalf of a student, then such person or persons is considered to be the parent or guardian for the purposes of §20 U.S.C. 1401(23).

## What Disabilities Are Covered Under IDEA?

Under IDEA, "a student with a disability" is a student who may have one or more of the following disabling conditions according to §20 U.S.C. 1401(3) and 1401(30):

## Autism

Autism means a developmental disability significantly affecting verbal and nonverbal communication and social interaction, generally evident before age 3, that adversely affects a student's educational performance. Other characteristics often associated with autism are engagement in repetitive activities and stereotyped movements, resistance to environmental change or change in daily routines, and unusual responses to sensory experiences. Autism does not apply to a student whose educational performance is adversely affected primarily because the student has an emotional disturbance.

## Deaf-Blindness

Deaf-blindness means concomitant hearing and visual impairments, the combination of which causes such severe communication and other developmental and educational needs that the affected person cannot be accommodated in special education programs for students solely with deafness or solely with blindness.

## Deafness

Deafness means a hearing impairment that is so severe that the student is impaired in processing linguistic information through hearing, with or without **amplification,** and that adversely affects a student's educational performance.

## Developmental Delay

A student with a developmental delay is one who, in physical development, cognitive development, communication development, social or emotional development, adaptive development, or any combination thereof

- Is so defined by the state and as measured by appropriate diagnostic instruments and procedures, and
- By reason thereof, needs special education and related services

## Emotional Disturbance

Emotional disturbance means a condition exhibiting one or more of the following characteristics over a long period of time and to a marked degree that adversely affects a student's educational performance:

- An inability to learn that cannot be explained by intellectual, sensory, or health factors
- An inability to build or maintain satisfactory interpersonal relationships with peers and teachers
- Inappropriate behavior or feelings under normal circumstances
- A general pervasive mood of unhappiness or depression
- A tendency to develop physical symptoms or fears associated with personal or school problems

Emotional disturbance includes schizophrenia. The term does not apply to students who are socially maladjusted.

## Hearing Impairment

Hearing impairment means a level of sensitivity in hearing, whether permanent or fluctuating, that adversely affects a student's educational performance but that does not meet the definition of deafness.

## Mental Retardation

Mental retardation means significantly subaverage general intellectual functioning, existing concurrently with **deficits** in **adaptive behavior** and manifested during the developmental period, that adversely affects a student's educational performance.

## Multiple Disabilities

Multiple disabilities means concomitant impairments (such as mental retardation and blindness or mental retardation and orthopedic impairment), the combination of which causes such severe educational needs that they cannot be accommodated in special education programs solely for one of the impairments. Multiple disabilities does not include deaf-blindness.

## Orthopedic Impairment

Orthopedic impairment means a severe physical condition that adversely affects a student's educational performance. The term includes impairments caused by a congenital anomaly, impairments caused by disease (e.g., poliomyelitis, bone tuberculosis), and impairments from other causes (e.g., cerebral palsy, amputations, and fractures or burns that cause contractures).

## Other Health Impairment

Other health impairment means having limited strength, vitality or alertness, including a heightened alertness to environmental stimuli, that results in limited alertness with respect to the educational environment, and that

- Is due to chronic or acute health problems such as asthma, attention deficit disorder or **attention deficit/hyperactivity disorder,** diabetes, epilepsy, a heart condition, hemophilia, lead poisoning, leukemia, nephritis, rheumatic fever, and sickle cell anemia
- Adversely affects a student's educational performance

## Specific Learning Disability

Specific **learning disability** means a disorder in one or more of the basic psychological processes involved in understanding or in using language, spoken or written, that may manifest itself in the imperfect ability to listen, think, speak, read, write, spell, or to do mathematical calculations, including conditions such as perceptual disabilities, brain injury, minimal brain dysfunction, **dyslexia,** and developmental **aphasia.**

Specific learning disability does not include learning problems that are primarily the result of visual, hearing, or motor disabilities, of mental retardation, of emotional disturbance, or of environmental, cultural, or economic disadvantage.

## Speech or Language Impairment

Speech or language impairment means a communication disorder, such as stuttering, impaired **articulation,** a language impairment, or a voice impairment, that adversely affects a student's educational performance.

## Traumatic Brain Injury

Traumatic brain injury means an acquired injury to the brain caused by an external physical force, resulting in total or partial functional disability or psychosocial impairment, or both, that adversely affects a student's educational performance. Traumatic brain injury applies to open or closed head injuries resulting in impairments in one or more areas, such as **cognition,** language, memory, attention, reasoning, abstract thinking, judgment, problem-solving, psychosocial behavior, physical functions, information processing, speech, and sensory, perceptual, and motor abilities. Traumatic brain injury does not apply to brain injuries that are congenital or degenerative or to brain injuries induced by birth trauma.

## Visual Impairment

Visual impairment means a level of acuity in vision that, even with correction, adversely affects a student's educational performance. The term includes both partial sight and blindness.

# Steps in the Special Education Process

# 1

# Step I

## The Prereferral Process

The prereferral process involves the identification, evaluation, and disposition of cases involving students who are **at-risk** students by a local school committee known as the Child Study Team. Further, some of these students identified as being at risk may be suspected of having an educational disabilities that would necessitate further interventions.

## What Are Child Study Teams?

A Child Study Team (CST) is a local school committee that uses a more global approach to the identification of at-risk students. In some schools, the Child Study Team is referred to by other names (for example, School Based Support Team, **Pupil Personnel Team**).

## What Is the Purpose of Child Study Teams?

The members of the Child Study Team work together in determining the possible **etiology** (cause), contributing factors, educational status, prognosis (outcome), and recommendations for the referred student. The reason for using a team approach is that it draws on many experts covering many fields and disciplines to review a student's case rather than rely on a single individual to determine all the factors. The overall purpose of the CST is to find the best educational resolution for each student's profile.

## Who Are the Members of the Child Study Team?

This Child Study Team is usually made up of the following individuals:

- *Administrator:* The administrator is usually the principal or assistant principal. He or she may bring to the meeting any prior experience with the student, a sibling, or family members.
- *Psychologist:* The psychologist may be able to contribute prior test results, outside professional reports that have been released to the school, conversations (with parent or guardian permission) with a therapist, psychiatrists, and so on who have had experience with the student, and observations of the student and any prior interactions or interviews with the student or family.
- *Nurse:* The nurse will be able to inform the CST of any medical information that may have a bearing on the case. The nurse should be able to provide measures of vision and hearing acuity tests, reports and results from the student's pediatrician or other health professionals, medications the student is taking if any, and any other medical information available.
- *Classroom teacher:* The classroom teacher will bring samples of work, informal test results, portfolio assessments (if applicable), **anecdotal records,** personal observations, summary of meetings with parents or guardians, observations of peer interaction, and so on.
- *Social worker:* If a social worker is on the CST, he or she may have had interactions with the family or other family members, results of a home visit, or experiences with the student if the student was in a group with the social worker.
- *Special education teacher:* The special education teacher may have information on prior educational testing, personal observations of the student, or **screening** results for the student.
- *Guidance counselor on the secondary level:* The guidance counselor will be able to provide report card grades dating back to kindergarten, achievement test scores as far back as possible, classroom teacher reports, aptitude test results, and impressions from personal involvement with the student and his or her family.

- *Reading teacher:* The reading teacher will provide any reading evaluations that may have been done on the student, experiences from remedial reading interventions (if applicable), screening results, and observations from any personal involvement with the student, siblings, or family members.
- *Speech and language pathologist:* The speech and language pathologist may bring screening test results, observations, and any interactions with the student, siblings, or parents or guardians.

## What Is a Referral to the Child Study Team?

Usually the first time a psychologist, special education teacher, or Child Study Team becomes aware that the student may have a problem is when the classroom teacher fills out a referral form. The major purpose of such a form is to alert other school professionals that the student is exhibiting difficulties in the classroom that may require further attention.

## Who Normally Makes a Referral to the Child Study Team?

The sources of referrals to the Child Study Team can originate from many sources, including but not limited to

- Parents and guardians
- Teachers
- School staff such as principal, speech therapist, school psychologist
- Private therapists
- Doctors
- The student himself or herself

## What Is Discussed at the Child Study Team Meetings?

In order to determine the best direction and options for a student, the team must first address many issues in order to zero in on the possible causes and type of problems being exhibited. The questions that are often asked may include but are not limited to

- What are the comments from past teachers?
- What is going on at home?
- What are the achievement test scores and what patterns do they reflect?
- What does the developmental history look like?
- When was the last time vision and hearing were checked?
- What symptoms are being exhibited by the student that are of concern at this time?
- What has the teacher tried that has worked?
- What has the teacher tried that does not seem to alleviate the symptoms?
- What are the student's present academic levels of functioning?
- What is the student's social behavior like?
- Have the parents or guardians been contacted?

## What Are the Options of the Child Study Team?

The options open to the Child Study Team depend on the case. Sometimes the CST may need further information not available at the time of the initial meeting. This may include

- *Educational screening:* This recommendation is chosen by the CST when a student's academic skill levels (reading, math, writing, and spelling) are unknown or inconsistent. A screening is not a formal evaluation but a series of short, brief measures that give the CST some basic academic knowledge on which to make other decisions (Pierangelo, 2004).

> According to the law—Sec. 300.302 of IDEA 2004—screening for instructional purposes is not evaluation. Further, the screening of a student by a teacher or specialist to determine appropriate instructional strategies for curriculum implementation shall not be considered to be an evaluation for eligibility for special education and related services.

- *Parent/guardian intake:* This may be used to gather further information not available in school records.
- *Classroom management suggestions:* This option may involve collaboration between the classroom teacher and various Child Study Team members, such as the school psychologist, to try to help alleviate the problems the teacher faces.
- *Consolidation of program:* Sometimes, especially on the secondary level, consolidating a student's program so that the student has less time in school may alleviate a problem.
- *Disciplinary action:* There may be times when the team will suggest some type of disciplinary action to remediate or temporarily contain the problem.

- *Referral to student protective agencies for possible neglect or abuse:* If the case before the CST is one in which abuse or neglect is suspected, then it is the legal responsibility to have the case investigated. Everyone on the CST is a mandated reporter and must report a case of suspected neglect and abuse to the proper agency.
- *Vision and hearing screening:* If the team feels that the student's vision or hearing needs to be screened to rule it out as a possible contributing factor, the team will either ask the nurse to do the screening or ask for a more comprehensive evaluation from an outside professional. How screening is handled varies from state to state and from district to district.
- *Referral for a special education comprehensive assessment:* In the case where the CST has tried every possible intervention available at the local school level and the student is still having serious issues, a formal referral for a comprehensive assessment can be made by the team.

## What Is a Prereferral Strategy Plan?

Before making a formal referral for special education assessment, the Child Study Team must suggest prereferral strategies. Prereferral strategies are attempts to alleviate any problems in case a referral for further special education intervention is not necessary.

## How Is the Determination of a Suspected Disability Made by the Child Study Team?

After the CST has exhausted all possible means of resolution and intervention, it may consider the following criteria (among others) as a basis for a suspected disability and a referral for a special education comprehensive assessment:

- A long-standing history of the problem
- A severe discrepancy between ability and **achievement** as indicated on standardized tests
- A severe discrepancy between ability and performance as indicated by informal assessments
- Lack of successful response to the prereferral strategy plan
- Behavioral manifestations suggesting a potential disability, such as processing problems
- An increase in the intensity, duration, and frequency of symptoms such as aggressive behavior, **distractibility,** or failing grades

## What Happens After the Child Study Team Determines That a Student May Have a Disability?

At this point, the CST team will make a formal referral to the multi-disciplinary team or the IEP Committee requesting a comprehensive special education assessment. Members of the CST will first meet with the parent or guardian to go over the reasons for such a recommendation and provide the documentation for such a referral, such as test scores, grades, observation information, or prereferral strategy plan.

# 2

# Step II

## Initial Referral for Special Education Services

Once the Child Study Team has determined that a student may have a disability, the team will make a referral for a comprehensive assessment. This assessment will be used along with other information to help determine the nature and type of the student's disability if one exists.

## What Is a Referral for Special Education?

A referral is nothing more than a form starting the special education process in a formal manner. It usually is initiated by the Child Study Team or the parent or guardian.

Sec. 300.301 of IDEA 2004 states

*(a) General. Each public agency must conduct a full and individual initial evaluation, in accordance with Secs. 300.305 and 300.306, before the initial provision of special education and related services to a student with a disability under this part.*

*(b) Request for initial evaluation. Consistent with the consent requirements in Sec. 300.300, either a parent/guardian of a student, or a public agency, may initiate a request for an initial evaluation to determine if the student is a student with a disability.*

*(Continued)*

(Continued)

> *(c) Procedures for initial evaluation. The initial evaluation—*
>
> > *(1) (i) Must be conducted within 60 days of receiving parent/ guardian consent for the evaluation; or*
> > *(ii) If the State establishes a timeframe within which the evaluation must be conducted, within that timeframe; and*
> > *(2) Must consist of procedures—*
> > > *(i) To determine if the student is a student with a disability under Sec. 300.8; and*
> > > *(ii) To determine the educational needs of the student.*
>
> *(d) Exception. The timeframe described in paragraph (c)(1) of this section shall not apply to a public agency if—*
>
> > *(1) The parent/guardian of a student repeatedly fails or refuses to produce the student for the evaluation; or*
> > *(2) when the evaluation will be completed.*
> > > *(i) A student enrolls in a school served by the public agency after the relevant timeframe in paragraph (c)(1) of this section has begun, and prior to a determination by the student's previous public agency as to whether the student is a student with a disability under Sec. 300.8.*
>
> (Authority: 20 U.S.C. 1414(a))

## Who Can Make a Referral for Special Education?

Any one of the following individuals can initiate a referral for evaluation and possible special education services with a written request:

- The student's parent or guardian or advocate or a person in a parent or guardian relationship with the student
- A classroom teacher
- Any professional staff member of the public or private school district
- A judicial officer
- A student on his or her own behalf if 18 years of age or older, or an emancipated minor
- The chief school officer of the state or that officer's designee responsible for welfare, education, or health of students

## In What Form Is This Referral Made?

A referral should be in written form and should be dated. This makes it official and gives the parent or guardian a start date on which the timelines will be based. A referral from the parent or guardian should include the reason for the referral and any details describing the problems their child may be having. The same should hold true for a judicial officer and student referrals. It is important to be clear about why the parents or guardians are referring their child.

A referral from a professional staff member, a physician, or the commissioner of education should include documentation of why a disability may exist and descriptions of attempts to **remediate** the student's behaviors or performance prior to the referral. All the above is important, especially the attempts that have been made prior to the referral. Remember that the district should try to keep the student in the **mainstream** and the documentation they provide at this step in the process should assure the parents or guardians and the student that the district has done everything possible to address the problems before initiating the referral process.

Referrals can initially be sent either to the building administrator or to the Individualized Education Program (IEP) Committee chairperson. In either case, both the administrator and the chairperson should have a copy of the referral as soon as possible. If the referral is not from a parent or guardian, the district must immediately inform the parent or guardian in writing that the student has been referred. The referral indicates that the person submitting the referral believes that the student may have a disability that adversely affects educational performance. A referral to the IEP Committee does not necessarily mean that the student has a disability. It signals that the student is having learning difficulties and that the person making the referral is concerned that the problem may be due to a disability.

## Is Parent or Guardian Consent Necessary for an Evaluation for Special Education?

The district by law needs the parent's or guardian's consent for an evaluation. A request for an evaluation should not be misinterpreted as an automatic decision that the student has a disability. When the district asks for the parent's or guardian's consent, it is a means of ensuring that the parents or guardians have full knowledge of the district's actions. For the district to involve the parents or guardians in the decision making is part of due process (**see Step V: Procedural Safeguards Under IDEA**). The parent or guardian will need to fully understand the reasons for an individual evaluation for special education.

Parents and guardians have the right to request an informal conference if they have any questions about the purpose or type of evaluation proposed or if they do not want their child evaluated. This conference may be held with the committee chairperson, building principal, or any other professional who will be part of the assessment team. The parent or guardian may even contact the board of education. The parent or guardian or the school may withdraw the IEP Committee referral within a specified period of time if the parent or guardian and the referring party agree to another plan that better suits the student's needs. If, however, they do not reach agreement on the student's evaluation, due process options are available (**see Step V: Procedural Safeguards Under IDEA**).

## What Is an Assessment Plan?

It should be noted here that when a student is referred for a comprehensive special education assessment, either an assessment plan or a parent or guardian release for testing is required by law. The parent or guardian release can be obtained in several ways and at different points in the process, as the school district's policy and procedures may determine. For instance,

- Some districts may send out a letter to the parent or guardian indicating that his or her child has been referred for a comprehensive special education assessment by the Child Study Team (CST). In this letter, the parent or guardian will be provided with an assessment plan outlining his or her rights (see the law at the beginning of this section) and asking them to sign and submit this assessment plan so that the team can begin the evaluation.
- In some cases the CST may be able to have the parent or guardian sign this release when they meet with the parent or guardian to discuss the team's decision and the reasons for the decision to make a formal referral for a comprehensive special education referral. If the parent or guardian signs a release at that time, then the CST will attach the permission for evaluation to the initial referral form for a comprehensive assessment.
- In some cases, the assessment plan and release for evaluation may form part of an initial parent or guardian intake with an **interdisciplinary team** (sometimes referred to as a multidisciplinary team) member who has asked the parent or guardian in to gather background data.

## Does the Parent or Guardian Have to Agree With the Referral for Special Education?

The answer here is no. The referral by the district is a legal suggestion that the district must make if it suspects that a student has a disability as defined under federal law, IDEA. If the parent or guardian does not agree, the school will try to hold meetings, first with the CST, then with other administrators, and finally with the IEP Committee, at which time the parent's or guardian's concerns and possible areas of resolution will be discussed. If no agreement can be reached, parents are afforded due process rights to explore.

# 3

# Step III

## The Individual Evaluation Process for Special Education

## What Is an Evaluation for Special Education?

At the conclusion of the referral process to the IEP Committee, an individual evaluation of the student will take place. This can occur only if the parent or guardian has given written permission. The evaluation will involve formal tests, informal assessment measures, observations, interviews, and other assessment measures deemed necessary by the assessment team. This will help the school determine whether the student has a disability and whether special services are required. The evaluation will also attempt to determine whether factors unrelated to the disability are affecting the student in school. The results of the evaluation will be used as a guide to develop the student's educational program. It will determine whether adjustments will have to be made to the student's educational program.

## What Are the Components of a Comprehensive Evaluation?

Numerous tests might be used by professionals in the evaluation. All the tests used to evaluate the student's suspected disability should be administered individually.

Most tests are either norm-referenced or criterion-referenced. **Norm-referenced tests** are tests that are standardized on groups of individuals. Such tests measure a student's performance relative to the performance of a group of individuals with similar characteristics. Tests which are administered at the district, state, or national level are usually norm-referenced.

**Criterion-referenced tests** measure a student's achievement or development relative to a specific standard. Such tests are especially useful for planning instruction or measuring curriculum content mastery because they can correspond closely to curriculum content and classroom instruction. Tests that are selected or developed and administered by the classroom teacher are generally criterion-referenced.

Specifically, comprehensive evaluation measures may include but are not limited to

- An individual psychological evaluation (when determined to be necessary by the interdisciplinary (also referred to as multi-disciplinary) team of general intelligence, instructional needs, learning strengths and weaknesses, social-emotional dynamics (Such evaluations will be completed by a licensed school psychologist.)
- A social history taken by either a social worker or a school psychologist
- A physical examination that includes specific assessments of vision, hearing, and health conducted either by the school physician or the student's own doctor
- An observation of the student in his or her current educational setting (This observation is conducted in the classroom, usually by another teacher, most likely a resource room or special education teacher.)
- An appropriate educational evaluation specifically pinpointing the areas of deficit or suspected disability including educational achievement, academic needs, learning strengths and weaknesses, vocational assessments, and possibly other measures
- Vocational assessments if the student is of age to be included in transition services to assess work-related skills and interests, which is completed by professional vocational or rehabilitation counselors, work study evaluators, or the guidance counselors
- An assessment in the student's native language if the student has little English proficiency (The evaluation should be in the student's native language.)

Inform the parent or guardian that these evaluations may lead to the development of an individualized educational program (**see Step VI: IEP Development**) and that the parent or guardian should work closely with the school to ensure that the evaluation is comprehensive and beneficial in determining his or her child's future educational needs. If the parent or guardian decides that evaluations recommended or completed by the school are not appropriate or sufficient, he or she may have the right to obtain an independent evaluation at the expense of the district unless the district initiates an impartial hearing showing that the district's evaluation was sufficient. If the impartial hearing officer determines that the district's evaluation was appropriate, the parent or guardian may still wish to obtain an independent evaluation, understanding that the district will not be responsible for the expense.

Sec. 300.304 Evaluation procedures.

*(a) Notice. The public agency must provide notice to the parent/guardians of a student with a disability, in accordance with Sec. 300.503, that describes any evaluation procedures the agency proposes to conduct.*

*(b) Conduct of evaluation. In conducting the evaluation, the public agency must—*
  *(1) Use a variety of assessment tools and strategies to gather relevant functional, developmental, and academic information about the student, including information provided by the parent/guardian, that may assist in determining—*
    *(i) Whether the student is a student with a disability under Sec. 300.8; and*
    *(ii) The content of the student's IEP, including information related to enabling the student to be involved in and progress in the general education curriculum (or for a preschool student, to participate in appropriate activities);*

  *(2) Not use any single procedure as the sole criterion for determining whether a student is a student with a disability and for determining an appropriate educational program for the student; and*

  *(3) Use technically sound instruments that may assess the relative contribution of cognitive and behavioral factors, in addition to physical or developmental factors.*

*(c) Other evaluation procedures. Each public agency must ensure that—*
  *(1) Assessments and other evaluation materials used to assess a student under this part—*
    *(i) Are selected and administered so as not to be discriminatory on a racial or cultural basis;*
    *(ii) Are provided and administered in the student's native language or other mode of communication and in the form most likely to yield accurate information on what the student knows*

*(Continued)*

(Continued)

*and can do academically, developmentally, and functionally, unless it is clearly not feasible to so provide or administer;*

*(iii) Are used for the purposes for which the assessments or measures are valid and reliable;*

*(iv) Are administered by trained and knowledgeable personnel; and*

*(v) Are administered in accordance with any instructions provided by the producer of the assessments.*

*(2) Assessments and other evaluation materials include those tailored to assess specific areas of educational need and not merely those that are designed to provide a single general intelligence quotient.*

*(3) Assessments are selected and administered so as best to ensure that if an assessment is administered to a student with impaired sensory, manual, or speaking skills, the assessment results accurately reflect the student's aptitude or achievement level or whatever other factors the test purports to measure, rather than reflecting the student's impaired sensory, manual, or speaking skills (unless those skills are the factors that the test purports to measure).*

*(4) The student is assessed in all areas related to the suspected disability, including, if appropriate, health, vision, hearing, social and emotional status, general intelligence, academic performance, communicative status, and motor abilities.*

*(5) Assessments of students with disabilities who transfer from one public agency to another public agency in the same academic year are coordinated with those students' prior and subsequent schools, as necessary and as expeditiously as possible, to ensure prompt completion of full evaluations.*

*(6) In evaluating each student with a disability under Sec. 300.304 through 300.306, the evaluation is sufficiently comprehensive to identify all of the student's special education and related services needs, whether or not commonly linked to the disability category in which the student has been classified.*

*(7) Assessment tools and strategies that provide relevant information that directly assists persons in determining the educational needs of the student are provided. (Authority: 20 U.S.C. 1414(b)(1)–(3), 1412(a)(6)(B))*

## How Should Parents and Guardians Go About Obtaining School Records on Their Children?

Before parents or guardians are brought in for an interview as part of this evaluation procedure, they may want to obtain any school records on their child in order to be prepared. Parents and guardians have a right to these records. A district might require a small payment for mailing or reproduction costs in providing such records.

The school usually has a wealth of information about each student scattered among a number of people and a number of records. The Freedom of Information Act guarantees a parent's or guardian's right to look at and make copies of any or all information on his or her child that is available within the school. In order to accomplish this, the parent or guardian may need to inform the principal orally and sometimes in writing that he or she wishes to look at all the records available on his or her child. The parent or guardian should be specific and tell the school which records and materials should be available for viewing at the meeting. Gathering this information may increase the parent's or guardian's own awareness of the student's needs, reduce the need for testing, and provide a very thorough picture of the student and the student's abilities and patterns. School records usually exist in several files within a school, which may include

- A permanent record folder usually filed in the main office
- The guidance counselor's file (at the secondary level), usually filed in the guidance office
- Psychological records, including results of evaluations, usually filed in a locked cabinet in the psychologist's office
- Health records, usually filed in the nurse's office
- Disciplinary records, usually filed in the principal's office
- Special education records, including copies of IEPs, evaluation results, and so on, usually filed either in the special education teacher's files or at central administration offices with the director of pupil personnel services
- Attendance records, usually filed in the school's main office, or in the attendance office at the secondary level

These files will comprise a variety of information that will contribute to the overall picture of the student:

- *Prior teacher reports:* Comments written on report cards may provide a different view of the student under a different style of teaching. Successful years with positive comments may be a clue for the parent or guardian to the student's learning style and may provide information about the conditions under which the student responds best. This is usually found in the permanent record folder.
- *Reports of prior interviews between the parent or guardian and the teacher:* The permanent record folder or psychologist's folder

may contain notes on prior conferences that can provide parents and guardians with information that is important for understanding the student's patterns and history.

- *Cumulative school record:* This file may contain information from standardized achievement test results, group IQ results, teacher comments dating back to kindergarten, records from previous schools, and individual reading test results. There is usually no rule on what must be kept in this folder.
- *Group IQ test information:* If a district administers such tests, this information is usually found in the permanent record folder. Many schools administer an IQ test. Within the past year or so the term *school abilities index* has replaced the term *IQ* (intelligence quotient).
- *Report card grades:* These materials can be reviewed for comments and patterns of productive and difficult years. Copies of these reports are usually placed in the permanent record folder.
- *Attendance records:* These records can be reviewed to determine the accuracy of statements about the student's lateness or absence. If a pattern of lateness or absence exists, then the reasons should be reviewed by the parent or guardian to rule out medical causes (hospital stays, illness), psychological causes (dysfunctional family patterns, school phobia, or the like), or social causes (such as peer rejection or isolation).
- *Prior teacher referrals:* Prior referrals from teachers may appear in the record when no action was taken because of time of year, delay in evaluation procedures, or other factors. If these referrals are on file, they may reveal useful information.
- *Medical history in the school nurse's office:* These records may give indications of visual or hearing difficulties that the administration may not have on file. The administration also may not have important information on illness, medication, allergies, and medical emergencies.

## What Should a Parent or Guardian Expect and Provide for the Parent/Guardian Intake or Interview?

The next step in the process used by the school may involve asking a parent or guardian to come in for a meeting to provide a complete social history, which can be regarded as a description of the family life situation. In some cases, this part of the process may not be possible because of the parent's or guardian's work restrictions, inability to obtain supervision of younger siblings, and so on.

- While the intake in many schools is done by the social worker, special education teacher, or psychologist, it is important that the parent or guardian understand the process if asked to provide information for the intake. There are several things to suggest to the parent or guardian before the meeting. School personnel should keep in mind that the parents and guardians have due process rights and no major decisions can be made without their input or permission.
- Parents and guardians should try not to view the school as an adversary even if they have experienced several negative school meetings over the years.
- Since the parent or guardian may be asked at the meeting to sign an assessment plan and release for testing, he or she should be offered information on the types of assessments used, the purpose of testing, and what the parent or guardian may gain from the process.
- The intake professional should make plain the purpose of the meeting and the steps that will be involved in the referral process once the parent or guardian gives permission to evaluate.
- The Director of Special Education should discuss and explain the procedures to be followed if the testing reveals the presence of an educational disability and the case needs to be reviewed by the IEP Committee. The parent's or guardian's understanding of what will happen is important and bears on the parent's or guardian's right to due process.
- The parent or guardian should clearly understand which individuals on the team will be seeing the information and the purpose for their review of the facts.

The evaluation process requires the parent/guardian intake to gather relevant past and present information that might have an impact on the student's present situation. At the intake, many questions may be asked about family history, developmental history, academic history, social history, and so on. If at any time the parent or guardian feels uncomfortable with a question, he or she should indicate a preference to not discuss the issue. A parent/guardian intake form should contain necessary but not intrusive questions. The questions should be specific enough to help in the **diagnosis** of the problem, but not so specific as to place parents and guardians in a vulnerable and defensive position. An example of a completed form follows.

**Example Intake Form**

*Identifying Data*

**Name of client**: Matthew Jones

**Address**: 12 Court Street

**Phone:** 675-7863

**Date of birth:** 3/4/97

**Age:** 9

**Brothers:** (names and ages) Brian, 15

**Sisters:** (names and ages) Karen, 4

**Mother's name**: Jill

**Father's name**: Ben

**Mother's occupation**: Medical technician

**Father's occupation**: Accountant

**Referred by**: Teacher

**Grade**: 4

**School**: Holland Avenue

*Developmental History*

**Length of pregnancy:** Full term—22-hour labor

**Type of delivery**: Forceps

**Complications:** Apgar score 7, jaundice at birth

**Long hospital stays**: None

**Falls or injuries**: None

**Allergies:** Early food allergies, none recently

**Medication:** None at present

**Early milestones:** (that is, walking, talking, toilet training)

According to parent, Matthew was late in walking and talking in comparison to brother. He was toilet-trained at 3. Parent added that he seemed to be slower than usual in learning things.

**Traumatic experiences**: None

**Previous psychological evaluations or treatment:** (Please explain reasons and dates.) None. However, parent indicated that it was suggested by first grade teacher, but the teacher never followed through.

**Any psychiatric hospitalizations?** No

**Sleep disturbances:** Trouble falling asleep, somnambulism at age 5 but only lasted a few weeks. Talks a great deal in his sleep lately.

**Eating disturbances**: Picky eater, likes sweets

**Last vision and hearing exams and results**: Last eye test in school indicated 20/30. Last hearing test in school was inconclusive. Parent has not followed through on nurse's request for an outside evaluation.

**Excessively high fevers**: No

**Serious childhood illnesses**: None

*Academic History*

**Nursery school experience**: Matthew had difficulty adjusting to nursery school. The teacher considered him very immature, and his skills were well below those of his peers. He struggled through the year.

**Kindergarten experience:** (adjustment, comments, etc.) Matthew's difficulties increased. According to parent, he had problems with reading and social difficulties. His gross and fine motor skills were immature.

**First grade through sixth grade:** (for example, teacher's comments, traumatic experiences, strength areas, comments)

According to past teachers, Matthew struggled through the years. He was a nice boy and polite and at times tried hard. But in grades 2 and 3 his behavior and academics began to falter. Teachers always considered referral but felt he might grow out of it.

**Subjects that presented the most difficulty**: Reading, math, spelling

**Subjects that were the least difficult**: Science

**Most recent report card grades:** (if applicable) Matthew has received mostly "needs to improve" on his report card.

*Social History*

**Groups or organizations**: Tried Boy Scouts but dropped out. Started Little League but became frustrated.

**Social involvement as perceived by parent/guardian**: Inconsistent. He does not seem to reach out to kids and lately he spends a great deal of time alone.

**Hobbies or interests**: Baseball cards, science

# What Occurs After the Comprehensive Assessment Is Completed?

Once the comprehensive assessment is completed by the multidisciplinary team, then the results will be shared with the CST and the parent or guardian. At that point, a case manager may be assigned to the case. This individual, who is usually a member of the CST, will be given the responsibility to gather all the information that will be presented to the IEP Committee for possible special education classification and placement. The parent or guardian should be made aware that a copy of this packet of information should be provided before any meeting with the IEP Committee. If a parent or guardian does not receive this packet, have him or her request it. The packet may contain the following information:

- District checklist
- Copy of original assessment plan signed by the parent or guardian
- Copy of the initial referral to the multidisciplinary team
- A copy of the educational report
- A copy of the psychological report
- A copy of the report from any other assessment area, that is, **occupational therapist,** speech and language therapist, psychiatrist
- Copy of the student's schedule
- Copies of the student's report cards
- Attendance records
- Teacher reports
- Disciplinary reports (if applicable)
- A medical form from the school nurse
- Copies of outside reports (if applicable)
- Group achievement test scores if available

This packet is then sent to the chairperson of the IEP Committee who will set up a meeting of the committee. The parent or guardian will be invited to this meeting by mail and can request a different date if not convenient.

# 4

# Step IV

## Eligibility for Special Education

## What Is an Eligibility Committee?

A recommendation is a statement developed by the Eligibility Committee that addresses the individual educational needs of the student. By law, parents and guardians are invited to Eligibility Committee meetings and encouraged to participate in developing the recommendation with the Eligibility Committee. The Eligibility Committee will use the evaluations completed by the designees and the district evaluators to decide whether the student meets criteria for a disability and is entitled to special education services.

If the student does not require special education, the Eligibility Committee will forward copies of the recommendation to the parent or guardian, the building administrator, and the board of education. It will state the Eligibility Committee's findings and should recommend what other educational services, such as speech and language improvement services, should be considered. The Eligibility Committee should determine what, if any, educationally related support services should be provided to the student.

If the student requires special education, then an IEP is developed by another committee called the IEP Committee. In some districts this is the same committee as the Eligibility Committee, while in other districts it may be a separate committee. The IEP will include the specific type of disability, describe the student's strengths and areas of need, list goals that the student should reach in a year's time (the **annual goals**), include short-term instructional objectives that represent a series of specific skills to be mastered, and identify the types of programs and services, including general education, that the student will receive. A copy of the recommendation will be sent to the board of education for approval. The parent or guardian will also be sent a copy of the IEP for his or her records. (**See Step VI: IEP Development** for more information on IEPs.)

## What Are the Responsibilities of the Eligibility Committee?

Some of the responsibilities of the district's Eligibility Committee are to

- Review and evaluate all relevant information on each disabled student
- Determine the least restrictive educational setting for any student who has been classified as having a disability
- Follow appropriate procedures and take appropriate action on any student suspected of having a disability
- Determine the suitable classification for a student suspected of having a disability
- Review at least annually the status of each disabled student residing within the district
- Evaluate the adequacy of programs, services, and facilities for the disabled students in the district
- Maintain ongoing communication in writing with parents and guardians on planning, modifying, changing, reviewing, placing, or evaluating the program, classification, or educational plan for a disabled student
- Advise the board of education on the status of and recommendations for all disabled students in the district

Most eligibility committees try to remain as informal as possible to reduce anxiety. This is crucial, since the parent or guardian may feel overwhelmed or intimidated.

## Who Are the Members of the Eligibility Committee?

Membership of the Eligibility Committee shall include school division personnel representing the disciplines providing assessments, the special education administrator or designee, and the parent(s) or guardian(s). At least one representative in the group must have either assessed or observed the student.

In determining whether a student has a specific **learning disability,** the group must include the student's regular teacher.

- If the student does not have a regular teacher, a regular classroom teacher qualified to teach a student of that age; or
- For a student less than school age, an individual qualified to teach a student of that age and at least one person qualified to conduct diagnostic examinations of students such as
  - a school psychologist
  - a speech-language pathologist
  - a teacher of specific learning disabilities, or
  - a teacher of remedial reading

## What Is the Role of the Parent/Guardian Member on the Eligibility Committee?

The parent/guardian member usually serves as a liaison and advocate for the parent or guardian, establishing contact prior to the meeting to reduce anxiety and alleviate any concerns that the parent or guardian may have. School personnel should also be in contact with the parent or guardian before the meeting to go over the process, rights, and what may take place at the meeting. At no time should anyone in contact with the parent or guardian before the meeting give the parent or guardian false hope, make promises, or second-guess the Eligibility Committee. What needs to be communicated are procedural issues and options, and the fact that it is the Eligibility Committee that will make the recommendation, not one individual. Further, the parent or guardian must be made aware of the rights he or she has and understand the right to due process if he or she does not agree with the Eligibility Committee's recommendation.

If the Eligibility Committee determines that the student is eligible for special education, the recommendations will describe the student's special and general educational program in detail. At this point, the parent or guardian will be asked to give consent before the program begins. Again, parents and guardians have the right to agree or disagree with the recommendation. No recommendation can be instituted without the approval of the parent or guardian (**later described in Step V: Procedural Safeguards Under IDEA**).

## What Is a Recommendation to the Eligibility Committee?

Once the evaluation process is completed, the Eligibility Committee will arrange to meet with the parent or guardian to discuss the results of the evaluations. Normally, the results of each evaluation is discussed by the individual who has completed the evaluation. This is an informal meeting, however, and its procedures will depend on district policy. The parent or guardian will receive a formal notice indicating the time and date of an Eligibility Committee meeting. Those attending will normally be

- A parent or guardian of a student with a disability in the district
- A physician (may be required only at the prior request of the parent or guardian)
- A school psychologist
- A district representative who provides, supervises, or administers special education
- The student's teacher, normally

The state may require members to include any professionals deemed necessary by the board of education, such as a guidance counselor, a social worker, or a special education teacher.

The parent or guardian has the right to bring persons of his or her choice, that is, a lawyer, advocate, friend, clergy, therapist, or other individuals who the parent or guardian feels would be helpful in the process.

## What Are the Procedures for Determining Eligibility?

The Eligibility Committee members making the decision on the student's eligibility shall work toward consensus. Although unanimity is not required the committee should try to be unanimous in its decision to show a united front on what their professional belief is about this child's needs. Regardless of the committee's decision, the school district would have to obtain parent or guardian consent for the initial eligibility determination. Thereafter, parent or guardian consent shall be secured for any change of identification.

The Eligibility Committee shall have a written summary that consists of the basis for making its determination of the eligibility of the student for special education and related services. This summary shall be signed by each Eligibility Committee member present. The written summary shall be maintained in the student's scholastic record.

The district should provide a copy of the documentation of the determination of eligibility to the parent(s) or guardian(s). The summary statement of the Eligibility Committee's essential deliberations shall be forwarded by the committee to the parents upon determination of eligibility. The summary statement may include other recommendations.

Each member of the Eligibility Committee shall certify in writing whether the report reflects his or her conclusions. If the group does not reach a unanimous decision and the report does not reflect a particular member's conclusion, then the group member must submit a separate statement presenting that member's conclusions.

## What Is Response to Intervention (RTI)?

According to the National Joint Committee on Learning Disabilities (2005), **response to intervention,** or RTI, is the practice of

- Providing high-quality instruction and **intervention** matched to student needs
- Using learning rate over time and level of performance to make important educational decisions

Although there is no single, widely used model for response to intervention, it is generally defined as a three-tier model that uses research-based interventions designed to help a student become more successful, rather than focusing on the student's lack of success.

The whole idea of RTI is to prevent students from developing more serious academic and behavior problems. The earlier we catch potential problems, the better the chance of students being successful.

A key element of an RTI approach is the provision of early intervention when students first experience academic difficulties, with the goal of improving the achievement of all students, including those who have a learning disability. In addition to the preventive and remedial services this approach may provide to at-risk students, it shows promise for contributing data useful for identifying learning disabilities. Thus, a student exhibiting (1) significantly low achievement and (2) insufficient RTI may be regarded as being at risk for a learning disability and, in turn, as possibly in need of special education and related services. The assumption behind this paradigm, which has been referred to as a dual discrepancy (Fuchs, Fuchs, & Speece, 2002), is that when provided with quality instruction and remedial services, a student without disabilities will make satisfactory progress.

# 5

# Step V

## Procedural Safeguards Under IDEA

## What Are Procedural Safeguards?

Parents and guardians have rights that apply to every aspect of the special education process. These are known as procedural safeguards. The State Education Agency (SEA) is required to provide notice of these procedural safeguards. There are laws and regulations that spell out those rights and the procedures that must be followed to ensure that students with disabilities receive a free appropriate public education (FAPE).

The regulations implementing IDEA include an entire section titled "Procedural Safeguards." Procedural safeguards are designed to protect the rights of parents and guardians and their child with a disability, as well as to give families and public agencies a mechanism for resolving disputes. Some procedural safeguards under IDEA 2004 are

- The right of parents and guardians to inspect and review their child's educational records
- The right of parents and guardians to obtain an independent educational evaluation (IEE)
- The right of parents and guardians to be given prior written notice on matters regarding the identification, evaluation, or educational placement of their child or the provision of FAPE to their child

- The right of parents and guardians and public agencies to request mediation and an impartial due process hearing on these matters (At a minimum, mediation must be available whenever an impartial due process hearing is requested.)
- The right of parents and guardians to receive a full explanation of all the procedural safeguards available under IDEA and the state's complaint procedures
- The right of parents and guardians and public agencies to appeal the initial hearing decision to the SEA if the SEA did not conduct the hearing
- The right of the student to remain in his or her present educational placement, unless the parent or guardian and the public agency agree otherwise, while administrative or judicial proceedings are pending
- The right of parents and guardians or public agencies to bring a civil action in an appropriate state or federal court to appeal a final hearing decision
- The right of parents and guardians to request reasonable attorney's fees from a court for actions or proceedings brought under the IDEA under the circumstances described in Section 300.513
- The right of parents and guardians to give or refuse consent before their child is evaluated or reevaluated
- The right of parents and guardians to give or refuse consent before their child is provided with special education and related services for the first time

## What Are Parents' and Guardians' Rights to Receive Notice?

Parents' and guardians' participation in their child's education is essential. They have a right to be involved in meetings about identification, evaluation, and educational placement of their student, as well as other matters relating to their child's free appropriate public education (FAPE). This also means that they have the right to receive prior written notice from the local educational agency (LEA) each time important decisions are made that affect their child's special education services and before those decisions are implemented, including the right to prior written notice from the LEA when they propose or refuse to initiate or change the identification, evaluation, or educational placement of the student or the provisions of FAPE for the student.

Prior written notice must also be provided in a language understandable to the general public and must be provided to the parent or guardian of a student with a disability in the parent's or guardian's native language or other mode of communication unless it is not feasible to do so. Also, if the parent or guardian is deaf or blind or has no written language, the notice must be translated by means with which the parent or guardian normally communicates (e.g., Braille, sign language, or spoken language). The LEA shall document in writing that all notice requirements have been met and that the parent or guardian understands the content.

## What Are Parents' and Guardians' Rights to Grant or Withhold Consent?

### Informed Consent

Informed consent is the parent's or guardian's written approval with signature of a proposed action. Complete information about the action must be given to the parent or guardian in his or her native language or other mode of communication. It is important that parents and guardians understand that their approval is voluntary and may be taken back at any time.

### Initial Evaluation

The LEA must have the parent's or guardian's informed written consent and signature before it can conduct an initial evaluation to determine if the student is eligible for special education and related services.

### Reevaluation

The LEA must normally have the parent's or guardian's informed written consent and signature before reevaluating the child. The LEA may, however, reevaluate the student without the parent's or guardian's written consent if the LEA can demonstrate that it has taken reasonable steps to get such consent and show that the parent or guardian has not responded.

### Initial Placement

The LEA must have the parent's or guardian's informed written consent and signature before the school district can initially place the student in a special education program or provide special education and related services to the student.

### Refusal

Parents and guardians have the right to refuse consent for an evaluation, a reevaluation, or the initial placement of their child in special education and related services. Parents and guardians also have the right to revoke (take back) their consent at any time before an activity begins even though they have previously agreed to that action. If parents or guardians revoke their consent, they must do so in writing and date and sign their revocation. Nonetheless, the LEA may seek to evaluate the student for special education services through mediation or a due process hearing if it believes it is necessary to provide FAPE for the student.

Upon completion of the evaluation process, if parents or guardians refuse to give consent for special education and related services for the student, then the school or LEA cannot provide these services for the student. If parents or guardians refuse or fail to respond to the request for consent for special education and related services for the student, then the school or LEA will not be considered to be in violation of the requirement to make FAPE available to the student, nor will the school or LEA be required to convene an IEP meeting or develop an IEP for the student.

In other words, parents' or guardians' written permission is required before the student is first evaluated or placed in special education and related services.

## What Are Parents' and Guardians' Rights for Evaluation, Reevaluation, and an Independent Educational Evaluation?

### Evaluation Procedures

A full and individual evaluation of a student must be completed to determine eligibility for special education services, before any special education services begin, or before the student is dismissed from services. An evaluation is not required, however, if the student is graduating with a high school diploma or has exceeded the age eligibility for FAPE. In these instances an LEA shall provide the student with a summary of his or her academic achievement and functional performance instead of an evaluation. Parents and guardians have the right to participate in meetings about the identification, evaluation, and educational placement to ensure the provision of FAPE to the student. The LEA uses a multidisciplinary team evaluation process to decide whether the student is a student with a disability and to determine his or her educational needs.

A student in special education must be reevaluated at least once every three years unless the parent or guardian and the school or LEA agree that a reevaluation is unnecessary. The multidisciplinary team may decide that no additional data are needed to determine whether the student continues to be eligible for special education and what his or her educational needs are. In this case, the LEA must notify the parent or guardian in writing of that decision and the reasons for it. Parents and guardians still have the right to request an assessment to determine whether their student continues to be eligible for IDEA services. But remember, the LEA is not required to conduct another assessment of a student unless the parent or guardian requests it.

## Independent Educational Evaluation (IEE)

An independent educational evaluation (IEE) is an evaluation that meets the same criteria as that of the LEA's evaluation by a qualified examiner who is not an employee of the LEA responsible for educating the student. A parent or guardian who disagrees with the evaluation completed by the LEA may ask for an IEE. The LEA may ask for a reason for requesting the IEE. The IEE is to be completed at public expense, consistent with the LEA's cost guidelines, unless the LEA believes the school system's evaluation is appropriate and initiates a due process hearing. If the hearing officer finds that the LEA's evaluation is appropriate, parents and guardians still have the right to an IEE at their own expense. This IEE too must be considered in making any educational decision about the provision of a FAPE to the student and may be used as evidence in a due process hearing. When it is a hearing officer who requests an IEE for the student, however, it will be conducted at public expense.

In other words, parents and guardians have the right to an IEE of their student. Parents and guardians may request from the LEA a list of public and private agencies qualified to conduct an IEE. Any IEE will have the same status as an evaluation completed by the school district unless the LEA determines that its standards for conducting an evaluation have not been met by the IEE.

The IEE is to be done at public expense, consistent with the LEA's cost guidelines, unless the LEA refuses in the belief that the school district's evaluation is appropriate and initiates a due process hearing that substantiates the LEA's position.

## Do Parents and Guardians Need to Inform the School District If They Intend to Seek an IEE?

Although it is often helpful to consult with the school district when seeking an IEE, parents and guardians are not required to inform the school district in advance. Their decision to consult or not to consult with the school district will have no bearing on their rights to seek reimbursement for the cost of the IEE.

## Is the School Required to Accept the Results of an IEE?

The school district must consider the results of any IEE, including ones paid for by the parent or guardian, when making decisions about a student's educational program. The school district is not, however, required to agree with or implement all or any of the results or recommendations of the IEE. Parents and guardians may also submit the results of an IEE as evidence at a due process hearing.

## How Do Parents and Guardians Find a Professional or Clinic to Conduct an IEE?

The school district must provide a list of qualified independent evaluators when a parent or guardian asks for an IEE.

## Are a Student's Records Confidential?

There are provisions under the IDEA (and other federal laws as well) that protect the confidentiality of a student's educational records. These safeguards address three issues: (1) the use of personally identifiable information, (2) who may have access to a student's records, and (3) parents' and guardians' right to request that their child's records be amended.

## Identifiable Personal Information

Personally identifiable information includes (1) the names of the student and the parent or guardian, (2) the address of the student, (3) a personal identifier number (such as the student's social security number or student I.D. number), or (4) a list of personal characteristics or other information that would make it possible to identify the student with reasonable certainty. With a number of exceptions, the parent or guardian must give consent before any identifiable personal information can be disclosed by the school system. The exceptions are specified by each state. Parents and guardians can obtain this information through their district's special education director or through the state's office of special education.

## Access to a Student's Educational Records Is Frequently a Concern of Parents and Guardians

IDEA guarantees parents and guardians the right to inspect and review all educational records relating to their child that the public agency collects, maintains, or uses for the identification, evaluation, and educational placement of their student and the provision of FAPE to the student. Should parents and guardians ask to review their child's records, the public agency must respond to the request without unnecessary delay and before any meeting on an IEP or a due process hearing involving the student, and in no case later than 45 days after the request has been made.

Parents and guardians also have the right to receive a response to their reasonable requests for explanations and interpretations of the records. They may ask the agency to provide them with a copy of their child's records, and the school may charge them a reasonable fee for making the copies, as long as this fee does not effectively prevent parents or guardians from exercising their right to inspect and review the records. Schools may not charge them for searching for or retrieving the records.

Parents and guardians have the right to have a representative inspect and review the records. Furthermore, they have the right to obtain from the school district or other participating agency a list of the types of educational records that are collected, maintained, or used by the agency and where these records are kept.

In keeping with the requirements of federal law, only certain individuals besides parents and guardians may have access to their child's records. These individuals may include, for example, teachers or officials of the school or state who have a legitimate educational interest in the records. The school or other participating agency is required by law to maintain a record of all parties who obtain access to a student's educational records collected, maintained, or used under IDEA (with the exception of parents and guardians and authorized employees of the agency). This record should include the name of the person who accessed the records, the date, and the purpose for which the person was authorized to use the records.

## The Right to Request That Records Be Amended

The right to request that records be amended is also given to parents and guardians under the law. If parents and guardians believe the information in their child's records is inaccurate or misleading or that information in the records violates their child's right to privacy or other rights, they may request that the agency that maintains this information amend it. The agency must then decide, within a reasonable period of time, whether to amend the information in accordance with the request. If the agency decides to refuse to amend the information as requested, it must inform them of this decision, as well as advise parents and guardians of their right to a hearing.

If parents and guardians decide to challenge the school district's or other participating agency's refusal through a hearing, they have the right to present evidence showing why they feel the information in their child's records should be amended. Parents and guardians may also, at their own expense, be assisted or represented by one or more individuals of their choice, including an attorney. The hearing must be conducted by an individual who does not have a direct interest in its outcome, and the educational agency or institution must make its decision in writing within a reasonable amount of time after the hearing. The decision must be based solely on the evidence presented at the hearing and must include a summary of the evidence and the reasons for the decision.

Should the result of the hearing be in the parent's or guardian's favor, the district or other participating agency must amend the information in the student's records accordingly and inform parents or guardians in writing that it has done so. If, however, the result of the hearing is that the information about the student is not inaccurate, misleading, or otherwise in violation of his or her privacy or other rights, then the agency must inform the parent or guardian of the right to place in the child's records a statement commenting on the information or setting forth any reasons they have for disagreeing with the decision. The district must then place their statement in the records and keep it there as long as the record or contested portion is maintained by the agency. If the record of the student (or the contested portion) is disclosed by the agency to any party, the explanation must also be disclosed to that party.

IDEA 2004 has an additional provision on educational records and the inclusion of disciplinary information in those records. A state may now require that a public agency include in the records of a student with a disability a statement of any current or previous disciplinary action taken against the student. This statement would be transmitted to the same extent that the disciplinary information is included in, and transmitted with, the student records of nondisabled students. This statement may include

- A description of any behavior engaged in by the student that required disciplinary action
- A description of the disciplinary action taken
- Any other information that is relevant to the safety of the student
- If the state adopts such a policy and the student transfers from one school to another, the transmission of any of the student's records must include both the student's current IEP and any statement of current or previous disciplinary action taken against the student.

## What Are Parents' and Guardians' Rights of Access to Their Child's Records?

Both the Family Educational Rights and Privacy Act (FERPA) and IDEA require that parents and guardians have access to their child's educational records. Requests to look at their child's records should typically be made to the building principal. If access is denied and parents or guardians are prevented from reviewing and inspecting originals of the records, they have the right to request copies of them. Parents and guardians may ask for a list of the types and locations of educational records collected, maintained, or used for providing educational services to their child. The LEA shall provide their child's educational records within a reasonable time after the parent's or guardian's request, in no case more than 45 days after the date of the request, or before any hearing requested by the parent or guardian or the LEA.

## Can Parents and Guardians See Their Child's Educational Records?

If a student is under 18 years of age, parents and guardians have the right to inspect and review the student's school records unless their rights have been terminated under state law.

## Can Anyone Else See a Student's School Records Without a Parent's or Guardian's Consent?

School district employees can access a student's educational records when they need to do so in order to perform their job responsibilities. If a student transfers to a different school district, the employees of the new district also have access to the student's school records. In addition, school districts are required by law to share information with certain government agencies and organizations conducting studies for, or on behalf of, educational agencies or institutions.

## Can Parents and Guardians Review Their Child's School Records?

The school district must provide parents and guardians with the opportunity to review their child's school records within ten school days of the request, or within three school days of their request if they need the information to prepare for an IEP meeting or to prepare for a due process proceeding.

## How Can Parents and Guardians Obtain a Copy of Their Child's School Records?

Parents and guardians have the right to receive one free copy of their child's records. The request for a copy of their child's school records must be submitted to the school district in writing. The school district may take up to five school days to provide them with a copy of the student's records. The school district may charge a fee for any additional copies of the student's school records that parents or guardians request.

## Do Parents and Guardians Have a Right to Review Their Child's Records When He or She Becomes an Adult Student?

Until a student reaches age 18, his or her parents or guardians have access to all educational records maintained by the school. After the transfer of rights to the student upon reaching the age of majority, parents and guardians have the right of access to their child's educational records only if they have their child's written consent for access unless they maintain their student as a dependent for tax purposes.

## What Can Parents and Guardians Do When They Disagree With Their School District's Decisions?

Parents and guardians have the right to disagree with the school's or district's decisions on their child's evaluation, IEP, or educational placements. Some situations in which the parent or guardian and school personnel should meet to resolve disagreements are when the parent or guardian

- Refuses consent for an evaluation or does not agree with the school's or district's evaluation of their child
- Disagrees with the IEP or portions of it and have said so in writing
- Believes that the child is not receiving appropriate special education and related services and is not making reasonable progress
- Thinks that additional services are needed
- Does not think that the educational placement is appropriate for the student

# What Options Are Available to Parents and Guardians When They Disagree With the School District's Decisions?

- *Discussion or conference with school staff.* Staff may include teachers, counselors, the principal, the director of special education, and even the superintendent. Talking openly and honestly with involved professionals may be an effective means of addressing and resolving a disagreement.
- *An IEP review.* Parents and guardians may request an IEP review at any time they feel that the services their child is currently receiving are inappropriate or insufficient, or if the child is not making progress. If their child has received an IEE, the IEP review conference would be an appropriate time to consider the results of that evaluation. The IEP process will be discussed in Step VI.
- *Mediation.* IDEA 2004 establishes mediation as a voluntary process that may be used in resolving disputes between public agencies and the parent or guardian of a student with a disability. Mediation is a dispute settlement process in which a qualified and impartial third person (called a mediator) tries to negotiate a solution or compromise for the dispute. The mediator will listen to the parties and encourage them to make concessions or compromises. See the section on mediation (below) for more information.
- *Due process hearing.* Parents and guardians may request a due process hearing if they do not agree with their child's identification, evaluation, educational placement, or any aspect related to the provision of FAPE to their child. An impartial third party, called a hearing officer, will listen to the evidence that you and the public agency present and will issue a decision that contains the relevant facts and the legal basis for the decision. See the section on due process in the next section for more information.
- *Complaint resolution procedures.* Any individual or organization may file a complaint alleging that the state or other participating agency has violated a requirement of IDEA. Complaints must be written and signed and must contain a statement that a public agency has violated a requirement of IDEA and the facts upon which the statement is based. See the section on complaint resolution procedures below for more information.

## What Is Mediation?

When a district and a parent or guardian have a dispute they are unable to resolve, they may seek to address their differences through mediation. Mediation is a cost-free, voluntary process through which an impartial third party helps parties experiencing a conflict reach a suitable agreement. IDEA encourages (but does not mandate) the use of mediation whenever a dispute arises in the identification, evaluation, placement, or provision of an appropriate program of a student with a disability.

The ultimate goal of mediation is to seek a written agreement that is mutually acceptable to both parties. Even if a formal agreement is not reached, mediation may be helpful in clarifying issues. The district should refrain from using the term *mediation* to refer to any district-level process for resolving disputes. When an impasse is reached with a parent or guardian, the district should suggest use of the state mediation system.

Both parties must agree to mediation and it cannot be used in place of a due process hearing. A neutral, trained mediator will facilitate the meeting to help the two parties resolve their disagreements. The mediator is not a decision maker; rather, he or she works to help parties find a solution agreeable to both sides.

The law requires that the mediation process meet certain specific conditions, as follows:

- Mediation must be voluntary on the part of both parties.
- Mediation may not be used to deny or delay a parent's or guardian's right to a due process hearing or to deny any other right under Part B of IDEA.
- Mediation must be conducted by a qualified and impartial mediator who is trained in effective mediation techniques.
- The state must maintain a list of individuals who are qualified mediators and knowledgeable in laws and regulations relating to the provision of special education and related services.
- If a mediator is not selected on a random (e.g., a rotation) basis from the list of mediators, then both parties must be involved in selecting the mediator and agree with the selection of the individual who will mediate.
- The state must bear the cost of the mediation process.
- Each session in the mediation process must be scheduled in a timely manner and held in a location convenient to the parties in the dispute.
- An agreement reached by the parties must be set forth in a written mediation agreement.
- Discussions that occur during the mediation process must be confidential. They may not be used as evidence in any subsequent due process hearings or civil proceedings. The parties to the mediation process may be required to sign a confidentiality pledge prior to the beginning of the mediation.

## What Is Due Process?

Due process is a way of ensuring fairness in making decisions about a student with a disability. If parents or guardians disagree with a proposed or refused action for their child's education, and if they cannot work out the problem with the school district, they may initiate due process in order to resolve the disagreement.

## What Is a Due Process Hearing?

A due process hearing involves an impartial third party—called a hearing officer—who hears the evidence and issues a decision based upon that evidence and the requirements of the IDEA. Parents and guardians have the right to initiate a due process hearing on any matter related to their child's identification, evaluation, or educational placement or on any aspect related to the provision of FAPE to their child. This person may not be an employee of the state agency or LEA involved in the education or care of the student, nor can this person have a personal or professional interest that would conflict with his or her objectivity in the hearing. It is important to note that mere payment by the public agency to this person for serving as a hearing officer does not make the person an employee of the agency.

Under IDEA 2004, when parents or guardians request a due process hearing, they (or their attorney) are also required to provide the public agency with notice (which is to remain confidential) that they are requesting such a hearing. The notice must include

- The name of the student
- The address of the student's residence
- The name of the school the student is attending
- A description of the nature of the problem for the student, including facts relating to the problem
- A proposed resolution of the problem to the extent known and available to the parent or guardian at the time

A public agency may not deny or delay the parent's or guardian's right to a due process hearing for failure to provide the notice described above.

When a due process hearing is initiated, the public agency must inform the parent or guardian of the availability of mediation as a means to resolve the dispute in question. The agency must also tell the parent or guardian of any free or low-cost legal (and other relevant) services available in the area, if they request such information.

The right to request a due process hearing, however, is not reserved solely for parents and guardians. The public agency also has the right to initiate a mediation process or a due process hearing if a parent or guardian refuses to give consent to the initial evaluation or reevaluation or the initial provision of special education and related services to their child, unless doing so would be inconsistent with state law on parent or guardian consent.

Any party to the due process hearing—including the parents or guardians—has the right to

- Be accompanied and advised by counsel (that is, an attorney) or by individuals with special knowledge or training in the problems of students with disabilities
- Present evidence and confront, cross-examine, and compel the attendance of witnesses
- Prohibit evidence from being introduced at the hearing that has not been disclosed to that party at least five business days before the hearing
- Obtain a written or, at the option of the parent or guardian, an electronic verbatim record of the hearing
- Obtain written or, at the option of the parent or guardian, electronic findings of fact and decisions

At least five business days before the hearing, each party must disclose to all other parties all evaluations of the student completed by that date and recommendations based on the offering party's evaluations (that is, the party that has requested the due process hearing) that the party intends to use at the hearing. A hearing officer may bar any party that fails to comply with this prohibition from introducing the relevant evaluation or recommendation at the hearing without the consent of the other party.

Parents and guardians have certain additional rights at a due process hearing, as follows:

- Parents and guardians have the right to have their child present at the hearing.
- If the hearing will involve oral arguments, the hearing must be conducted at a time and place that is reasonably convenient to the parents or guardians and their child.
- Parents and guardians have the right to open the hearing to the public.
- The record of the hearing and the findings of fact and decisions must be provided at no cost to the parent or guardian.

At the hearing, the arguments and evidence of both the parent or guardian and the public agency are presented before the impartial hearing officer, who will make a decision on the matters at issue. The due process hearing must be completed and a copy of the decision mailed to the parent or guardian and the public agency within 45 days of their request for the hearing; the hearing officer may, however, grant a specific extension of time at the request of either party to the due process procedure. The decision is considered final, unless one of the parties to the hearing appeals the decision to the State Education Agency (SEA). Appeal to the SEA is available only if the SEA did not conduct the hearing.

If the hearing decision is appealed, the SEA must conduct an impartial review of the hearing, which involves examining the entire hearing record, ensuring that the procedures at the hearing were consistent with the requirements of due process, and seeking additional information, if necessary. If the reviewing official wishes to, he or she can afford both parties the opportunity to present oral or written arguments or both. The hearing officer must then make an independent decision and give a copy of the written or, at the officer's option, electronic findings of fact and decisions to the parties. The SEA must ensure that the entire process—from the initial receipt of the request for an impartial review to the rendering of a final decision and the mailing of that decision to each party—is completed in 30 days or less. The reviewing officer may grant specific extensions of time beyond the 30 days at the request of either party.

A parent or guardian or a public agency that disagrees with an initial hearing decision for which no SEA-level appeal is available, or any party aggrieved by the findings and decisions under the impartial review described above, has the right to bring a civil suit on the subject of the complaint presented as part of the due process hearing. It is important to realize, however, that civil actions can become quite costly and are certainly frustrating and time consuming.

## What Options Are Available to Parents and Guardians If They Want to Put Their Child in a Private School?

Parents and guardians always may remove their child from the public school and enroll him or her in a private school at their own expense. The law does not require an LEA to pay for the cost of educating, including special education and related services, a student at a private school or facility if that agency made FAPE available to the student and the parents or guardians chose to place the student in the private school or facility. Disagreements between a parent or guardian and a public agency on the availability of a program appropriate for the student may arise. As was discussed above, parents or guardians and public agencies have many means of resolving such disputes, including meetings and conferences and more formal proceedings such as mediation and due process.

If parents or guardians decide to place their child in a private school and they want the public agency to pay for the cost of the private school education, certain provisions of law come into play. One relates to the question of whether the public agency made FAPE available to the student, which will be a deciding factor in whether the agency must reimburse the parent or guardian for the cost of the private school education. If the parent or guardian enrolls the student in a private preschool, elementary school, or secondary school without the consent of or a referral by the agency, a court or hearing officer may still require the agency to reimburse the parent or guardian for the cost of that enrollment if the court or hearing officer finds (1) that the public agency had not made FAPE available to the student in a timely manner prior to the private school enrollment, and (2) that the private placement is appropriate. Another important provision is that the cost of the reimbursement may be reduced or denied for a number of reasons:

- If, at the most recent IEP meeting that the parent or guardian attended prior to removing their child from the public school, the parent or guardian did not inform the IEP Committee that they were rejecting the placement proposed by the public agency, including stating their concerns and their intent to enroll their child in a private school at public expense; or
- If, at least 10 business days (including any holidays that occur on a business day) prior to removing their child from the public school, the parent or guardian did not give written notice to the public agency of the information described above.

The cost of reimbursement may also be reduced or denied

- If, prior to the removal of the student from the public school, the agency informed the parent or guardian of its intent to evaluate their child (including a statement of the purpose of the evaluation that was appropriate and reasonable), but the parent or guardian did not make their child available for the evaluation; or
- If judicial proceeding actions taken by the parent or guardian have been unreasonable.

There are exceptions to these provisions, of course. The cost of reimbursement may not be reduced or denied for failure to provide the notice above if

- The parents or guardians are illiterate and cannot write in English
- Providing the notice as required by law would likely result in physical or serious emotional harm to their child
- The school prevented the parent or guardian from providing the notice, or
- The parent or guardian had not received notice that they were required to provide the public agency with notification of their intentions as described above

Thus, the parents or guardians may be able to secure reimbursement for the cost of their child's private school enrollment if the above conditions are met. (For example, a court or hearing officer finds that the public agency did not make FAPE available to the student and that the private school placement is appropriate; the parent or guardian notified the IEP team or the public agency of the intention to remove his or her child from the public school and place the child in a private school at public expense.) In any event, parents and guardians always have the option of placing the student in a private school and paying for such placement themselves.

# What Can the Public Agency Do If Parents or Guardians Do Not Consent to Their Student's Initial Evaluation, Reevaluation, or Initial Provision of Special Education and Related Services?

When parents or guardians refuse consent for an initial evaluation or reevaluation of their child or the initial provision of special education and related services, the agency may continue to pursue the evaluation or the provision of services through the mediation or due process procedures specified within the law, except to the extent that doing so would be inconsistent with state law on parent or guardian consent. Some states have policies that would prohibit the agency from overriding a parent's or guardian's refusal to consent. If so, the agency must follow the requirements of state law and, thus, may have no recourse but to not evaluate the student under IDEA or to not provide services to the student.

If no state law applies to a parent's or guardian's consent, the public agency may follow federal law and utilize either the due process or mediation procedures of IDEA to secure the initial evaluation or the initial provision of special education and related services.

In this case, the public agency must notify the parent or guardian of its intended actions (that is, to pursue mediation or a due process hearing). Parents and guardians may choose to participate in the mediation process, which is voluntary, and they have rights with respect to due process hearings (both mediation and due process are discussed further in other chapters).

The only exception to the above requirements for consent is a specific provision in the case of parents or guardians who fail to respond to a request for a reevaluation of their child. In this instance, informed parent or guardian consent is not necessary if the agency can demonstrate that it has taken reasonable measures to obtain that consent and the student's parent or guardian has failed to respond. (Note that this provision applies only in the case of reevaluation and only when parents and guardians fail to respond, as opposed to expressly refusing consent.) The regulations describe "reasonable measures," which means that the public agency must have a record of its attempts to secure parents' or guardians' consent to the reevaluation of their child, such as

- Detailed records of telephone calls made or attempted and the results of those calls
- Copies of correspondence sent to the parent or guardian and any responses received
- Detailed records of visits made to the parent's or guardian's home or place of employment and the results of those visits

# 6

# Step VI

## IEP Development

## What Is an Individualized Education Program (IEP)?

An IEP is a written statement for a student with a disability that is developed, reviewed, and revised in a meeting of a Committee on Special Education, Subcommittee on Special Education, or Committee on Preschool Special Education. The IEP is the tool that ensures that a student with a disability has access to the general education curriculum and is provided the appropriate learning opportunities, accommodations, adaptations, specialized services, and supports the student needs to progress toward achieving the learning standards and to meet the needs related to his or her disability.

Each student with a disability must have an IEP in effect by the beginning of each school year. Federal and state laws and regulations specify the information that must be documented in each student's IEP, including the classification of a student's disability, a description of the student's individual needs, the student's goals for the school year, and the special education services that will be provided to the student in the least restrictive environment.

# What Is the Purpose of an IEP?

The IEP is a written record of the decisions reached by the team members at the IEP meeting. The IEP serves many purposes:

- The IEP is the heart of IDEA 2004 and serves as a communication vehicle between a parent or guardian and the district.
- The IEP meeting enables parents and guardians and school personnel, as equal participants, to decide what the student's needs are, what services will be provided to meet those needs, and what the anticipated outcomes may be.
- The IEP process provides an opportunity for resolving any differences between the parents or guardians and the agency over the special education needs of a student with a disability: first, through the IEP meeting, and second, if necessary, through the procedural protections that are available to parents and guardians.
- The IEP sets forth in writing a commitment of resources necessary to enable a student with a disability to receive needed special education and related services.
- The IEP is a compliance and monitoring document that may be used by authorized monitoring personnel from each governmental level to determine whether a student with a disability is actually receiving the free appropriate public education (FAPE) agreed to by the parent or guardian and the school.
- The IEP serves as an evaluation device for determining the student's progress toward the projected outcomes.
- The IEP anchors an effective process that engages parents or guardians and school personnel in a meaningful discussion of the student's educational needs.

The IEP is not, however, a performance contract or a guarantee by the district or the teacher that a student will progress at a specified rate. But the district must ensure that all services set forth in the student's IEP are provided, and it is also obligated to make good-faith efforts to assist the student in achieving his or her IEP goals and objectives.

The IEP can be more than an outline and management tool of the student's special education program. It should be an opportunity for parents or guardians and educators to work together as equal participants to identify the student's needs, what will be provided to meet those needs, and what the anticipated outcomes may be. It is a document that is revised as the needs of the student change. The IEP is a commitment in writing of what resources the school agrees to provide. Also, the periodic review of the IEP serves as an evaluation of the student's progress toward meeting the educational goals and objectives. Finally, the IEP serves as the focal point for clarifying issues and cooperative decision-making by parents or guardians, the student, and school personnel in the best interest of the student. For all these reasons, the IEP is the cornerstone of special education.

# Who Develops the IEP?

An IEP can be developed or revised only by the Committee on Special Education, Subcommittee on Special Education, or Committee on Preschool Special Education. The committee is required to include certain individuals who know the student and his or her individual needs and who can commit the resources of the school to address the student's needs.

To develop an appropriate IEP for the student, a group of individuals with the knowledge of the student and expertise in the curriculum and resources of the school must come together, and the process for discussion and decision making needs to be effective and efficient. Information about the student's strengths, interests, and individual needs gathered from parents or guardians, teachers, the student, related service providers, and evaluations and observations are the foundation upon which to build a program that will result in effective instruction and student achievement. Each member of the multidisciplinary team that makes up the Committee on Special Education, Subcommittee on Special Education, or Committee on Preschool Special Education brings information and a unique perspective to the discussion of the student's needs and has an important role and responsibility in contributing to the discussion and the recommendations for the student.

Each committee has a chairperson who has certain responsibilities under the law and regulations. The chairperson of the Committee on Preschool Special Education must be the school district representative. The required members of the committee include the following:

## Parents or Guardians of the Student

The parents or guardians of a student with a disability are expected to be equal participants along with school personnel in developing, reviewing, and revising the IEP for their child. This is an active role in which the parents or guardians

- Provide critical information on the strengths of the student and express their concerns for enhancing the education of their child

- Participate in discussions about the student's need for special education and related services and supplementary aids and services
- Join with the other participants in deciding how the student will be involved and progress in the general curriculum and participate in state and district assessments and what services the agency will provide to the student and in what setting

Parents and guardians are important team members who can

- Verify the accuracy of personal identifying information
- Provide information and observations about the level of the student's functioning in his or her home environment and community
- Provide information on the student's medical status
- Participate in developing educational goals and objectives based on the present level of academic achievement of functional performance and identified needs
- Participate in determining the special education and related services to be provided
- Participate in identifying an appropriate educational program for the student

Though parents and guardians are expected to be equal partners at the IEP meeting, writing IEPs or participating at IEP meetings is a new experience for many families. Information could be shared with parents or guardians throughout the evaluation process and prior to IEP notification on what will be discussed at the meeting, questions to consider, transition questionnaires, and so on. This would enhance parents' or guardians' readiness to share their wishes (that is, goals) for their child, as well as to contribute to the determination of the student's needs and present levels of performance. Please remember that all information sent to parents and guardians must be in their native language. Districts must arrange for interpreters for parents or guardians when necessary.

## Not Less Than One General Education Teacher of Such Student (If the Student Is, or May Be, Participating in the General Education Environment)

Very often, general education teachers play a central role in the education of students with disabilities and have important expertise in the general curriculum and the general education environment.

Thus, a general education teacher must, to the extent appropriate, participate in the development, review, and revision of the student's

IEP, including assisting in (1) the determination of appropriate positive behavioral interventions and strategies for the student and (2) the determination of supplementary aids and services, program modifications, and supports for school personnel that will be provided for the student.

The teacher need not be required to participate in all decisions made as part of the meeting or to be present throughout the entire meeting or attend every meeting. (The student's needs and the purpose of the specific IEP Committee meeting will determine when the teacher's participation is necessary and appropriate.) For example, the general education teacher who is a member of the IEP team must participate in discussions and decisions about how to modify the general curriculum in the regular classroom to ensure the student's involvement and progress in the general curriculum and participation in the general education environment.

Circumstances may, however, make it unnecessary for the general education teacher to participate in discussions and decisions on, for example, the **physical therapy** needs of the student if the teacher is not responsible for implementing that portion of the student's IEP.

In determining the extent of the general education teacher's participation at IEP meetings, public agencies and parents or guardians should discuss and try to reach agreement on whether the student's general education teacher who is a member of the IEP team should be present at a particular IEP meeting and, if so, for what length of time. The extent to which it would be appropriate for the general education teacher member of the IEP team to participate in IEP meetings must be decided according to the case at hand.

## Not Less Than One Special Education Teacher, or Where Appropriate, Not Less Than One Special Education Provider of the Student

The special educator on the committee can be either the student's special education teacher, or the student's special education service provider, such as a speech therapist, if the related service is considered specially designed instruction. If the student is being considered for special education for the first time, the role of the special education teacher could be filled by a teacher qualified to provide special education for those with the disability that the student is suspected of having. Occupational therapists, physical therapists, and guidance counselors cannot fill the role of the special education teacher or service provider on the IEP team, since these individuals do not provide specially designed instruction.

In deciding which teacher should participate, the district may wish to consider the following possibilities:

- For a student with a disability who is receiving special education, the teacher could be the student's special education teacher. If the student's disability is a speech impairment, the teacher could be the speech-language pathologist.
- For a student with a disability who is being considered for placement in special education, the teacher could be a teacher qualified to provide education in the type of program in which the student may be placed.

## An Individual Who Can Interpret the Instructional Implications of the Evaluations

At least one individual must participate in the committee meeting who can provide information on the results of the student's individual evaluation report and assist the committee in identifying the implications of those results for the instruction of the student. This individual may be a member of the committee who is also serving as the general education teacher or special education teacher or related service provider of the student, the school psychologist, the representative of the school district, or a person having knowledge of the student or special expertise in the suspected disability when such member is determined by the school district to have the knowledge and expertise to fulfill this role on the committee.

## School District Representative

The school district representative must be someone who is qualified to provide or supervise special education and who is knowledgeable about the general education curriculum and the availability of resources of the district. The school district representative brings knowledge of the continuum of special education supports and services and should have the authority to commit the resources of the school and to ensure that whatever services are set out in the IEP will be provided.

The individual who meets these qualifications may be the same individual who is appointed as the special education teacher or related service provider of the student or the school psychologist on the committee. The chairperson of the Committee on Preschool Special Education must be the school district representative on the committee.

Each district may determine the specific staff person who will serve as its representative in a particular IEP meeting, as long as the person meets the following criteria:

- Is qualified to provide, or supervise the provision of, specially designed instruction to meet the unique needs of students with disabilities

- Is knowledgeable about the general curriculum
- Is knowledgeable about the availability of the resources of the public agency

## Individuals With Knowledge of the Student or Special Expertise in the Suspected Disability

In addition to the other required members, parents or guardians and school personnel have the option to include other individuals who have knowledge or special expertise that can be helpful in designing and monitoring the student's IEP. This is important to ensure that the committee includes the input of those persons who can add to the discussion of the student's needs and recommendations for supports and services. Such individuals could include, for example, a school nurse, a physical therapist or other related service provider, the student's private counselor, a **paraprofessional** working with the student, a student's athletic coach, a family member or family friend who knows the student and who can assist the parents or guardians. The determination of the knowledge or special expertise of any such individual is made by the party (parents or guardians or school) who invited the individual to be a member of the committee.

## Other Agency Representatives

- When the purpose of the meeting is to discuss transition services, other agency representatives are invited to discuss their role in supporting the student in school or afterschool activities. If an agency invited to send a representative to a meeting does not do so, the district must find other ways to involve the other agency in the planning of any transition services.
- When a student is or may be attending a private school or facility, a representative of that school or facility must be invited to participate in the student's committee meetings. A representative is also invited from a facility operated by another state department or agency (such as the Office of Mental Health or the Office of Student and Family Services) where the student is residing. If the private school or facility representative cannot attend, the school district must use other methods to ensure participation by the private school or facility, possibly by individual or conference telephone calls.
- Other members of the Committee on Preschool Special Education include the representative of the municipality and, for certain students when transitioning from early intervention services to the Committee on Preschool Special Education, a representative of the county's early intervention program.

## Whenever Appropriate, the Student With a Disability

If a purpose of an IEP meeting for a student with a disability will be the consideration of the student's transition service needs, the school district must invite the student and, as part of the notification to the parents or guardians of the IEP meeting, inform the parents or guardians that the agency will invite the student to the IEP meeting.

If the student does not attend, the school district must take other steps to ensure that the student's preferences and interests are considered.

Student participation in the IEP can be a significant step in assisting students to become their own advocates. As students prepare for the move from school to adult life, they will need opportunities to practice the skills necessary in situations where self-advocacy will be important.

Naturally, this is not accomplished by simply inviting the student to the IEP meeting. Activities designed to engage the student in the IEP process to be a full participant in the meeting include

- Reviewing assessment information, especially career or vocational assessments, prior to the meeting
- Examining academic progress
- Participating in long-range planning
- Establishing goals in employment, education, independent living, and community/participation after finishing school
- Exploring post–high school education and training programs
- Researching options available through adult service agencies
- Brainstorming strengths and needs
- Leading some of the discussion at the IEP meeting

# If a Student With a Disability Has Several General Education Teachers, Must All of Them Attend the IEP Meeting?

No. The IEP team need not include more than one general education teacher of the child. If the participation of more than one general education teacher would be beneficial to the child's success in school (for example, as a means of enhancing the child's participation in the general curriculum), it would be appropriate for them to attend the meeting.

Even if not all the teachers participate, the local educational agency is strongly encouraged to seek input from all the teachers who will not be attending. In addition, the local educational agency must ensure that each general education teacher (as well as each special education teacher, related services provider, and other service provider) of an eligible child has access to the child's IEP and is informed of his or her specific responsibilities related to implementing the IEP and of the specific accommodations, modifications, and supports that must be provided to the child.

Even if a guidance counselor is certified as a general education teacher, she or he cannot fill the role of general education teacher at the IEP meeting. This role must be filled by the child's general education teacher.

# What Content Must Be Included in a Student's IEP?

Under IDEA 2004, the IEP must address all of a student's identified special education and related service needs based on need, not the disability. The usual matters covered follow:

## A Statement of the Student's Present Level of Academic Achievement of Functional Performance

The IEP team reviews the existing evaluation data on the student, including information and concerns shared by the parents or guardians. The team also reviews any other current pertinent data related to the student's needs and unique characteristics, such as information provided by parents or guardians, anticipated progress toward desired outcomes after finishing school, current classroom-based assessments, the most recent reevaluation, input from the student's special and general education teachers and service providers, and, as appropriate, the results of the student's performance on statewide and districtwide assessments.

Statements of the student's present level of academic achievement of functional performance in an area of need include how a student's disability affects his or her involvement and progress in the general education curriculum (that is, the same curriculum as for students without disabilities). For preschool students, present levels of performance describe how the disability affects the student's participation in age-appropriate activities. The IEP for every student with a disability, even those in separate classrooms or schools must address how the student will be involved and progress in the general education curriculum. The statement should accurately describe the effect of the student's disability on the student's performance in each area of education that is affected.

## A Statement of Secondary Transition Service Needs for Students

It is crucial for IEP teams to begin planning for a student's intended outcomes for adult life while the student is still in school. A statement of the transition service needs of the student under the applicable components of the IEP that focus on the student's course of study (such as participation in drivers' education courses, a vocational education program, or general education curriculum), must be included in the IEP by the student's sixteenth birthday, or earlier if determined appropriate by the IEP team. More on transition services will be discussed in Step IX.

## Transfer of Rights to the Student

At least one year before the student reaches the age of majority (age 18), the IEP must begin to include a statement that the student has been informed of those rights under IDEA 2004 that will transfer to the student on reaching the age of majority.

## Special Considerations

In consideration of any particular needs of the student, the IEP team needs to consider what the law calls special factors:

- If the student's behavior interferes with his or her learning or the learning of others, the IEP team will consider strategies and supports to address the student's behavior.
- If the student has little proficiency in English, the IEP team will consider the student's language needs as they relate to his or her IEP.
- If the student is blind or visually impaired, the IEP team must provide for instruction in Braille or the use of Braille, unless it determines after an appropriate evaluation that the student does not need such instruction.
- If the student is deaf or hard of hearing, the IEP team will consider his or her language and communication needs. This includes the student's opportunities to communicate directly with classmates and school staff in his or her usual method of communication (for example, sign language).
- The IEP team must always consider the student's need for assistive technology devices or services.

## Statewide or Districtwide Achievement Testing

The IEP must include a statement of the accommodations that are necessary to measure the academic achievement and functional performance of the student as well as to participate in statewide and districtwide assessments. It is expected that all students, including students with disabilities, will participate in the statewide norm-referenced and criterion-referenced assessments. For districtwide assessments, if the IEP team determines that the student will not participate in the regular assessments, the IEP must state why that assessment is not appropriate for the student and include a statement of how the student will be assessed.

## Progress Toward Goals

The IEP must include a statement of how parents and guardians will be informed of their child's progress toward the annual goals and the extent to which that progress is sufficient to enable the student to achieve the IEP goals by the end of the IEP period. Parents and guardians of students with disabilities must be informed of progress at least as often as parents and guardians of students without disabilities.

## Measurable Annual Goals—Including Academic and Functional Goals—and Short-Term Objectives or Benchmarks

The academic and functional goals should focus on the learning and behavioral problems resulting from the student's disability and be aligned with state and district performance standards. They should address the needs that are summarized in the statement of the student's present levels of academic achievement and functional performance. For those students taking alternate assessment, there should be at least one goal, with corresponding objectives or benchmarks, for each area of need.

The goals and objectives or benchmarks provide a mechanism for determining whether the student is progressing in the special education program and the general education curriculum, and whether the placement and services are appropriate to meet the student's identified educational needs (20 U.S.C. § 1414(d)(1)(A)(i)(II)).

- *Measurable annual goals.* A goal is a measurable statement that describes what a student is reasonably expected to accomplish from the specialized educational program during the school year.
- *Short-term objectives or benchmarks.* The short-term objectives or benchmarks derive from the annual goals but represent smaller, more manageable learning tasks a student must master on the way to achieving the goals. The purpose of short-term objectives and benchmarks is to enable families, students, and teachers to monitor progress during the year and, if appropriate,

revise the IEP consistent with the student's instructional needs. They describe how far the student is expected to progress toward the annual goal and by when. In most cases, at least two objectives or benchmarks should be written for each annual goal. Progress on each short-term objective or benchmark should be documented.

## A Statement of Program Modifications and Support for School Personnel

The IEP must include program modifications or accommodations for the student and support that will be provided to school personnel to allow the student to

- Advance appropriately toward attaining the annual goals
- Be involved and progress in the general education curriculum and participate in extracurricular and other nonacademic activities
- Be educated and participate with other students with disabilities and nondisabled students

## Need for Extended School Year

Consideration of the need for an extended school year must be documented. If it is determined that a student requires an extended school year, it must be included in the IEP. The information used to support the determination should be referenced. An extended school year is not the same as summer school.

## A Statement of the Specific Special Education, Supplementary Aids, and Services to Be Provided to the Student Based on Peer-Reviewed Research to the Extent Practicable

The statement of services contained in the IEP must include the following information:

- All the specific special education and related services needed by the student in order to receive an appropriate education (e.g., **itinerant** program supervision, speech and language pathology services, assistive technology services, transition services, counseling services, physical therapy services)
- Supplementary aids and services, based on peer-reviewed research to the extent practicable must be provided to the student, or on behalf of the student

- The total amount of service required by the student per week
- The frequency of on-site program review by each itinerant service provider
- The amount and frequency of program supervision by certified special education staff
- The amount and frequency of counseling services

## Projected Starting Date and Anticipated Frequency, Duration, and Location of Services

- The projected starting date and anticipated frequency, duration, and location of services (and modifications) must be indicated for each special education and related service.
- The date must include the month, day, and year and extend no more than a year from the date of the meeting.
- The location refers to the type of environment that is the appropriate place for the provision of the service (such as the regular classroom or resource room).
- The total time that a student with a disability spends receiving general education, special education, and related services should equal the total amount of time the student spends in school.

## The Extent to Which the Student Will *Not* Be Able to Participate in General Education Programs

The IEP must include a statement of the extent, if any, to which the student will not participate in the regular classroom, general education curriculum, extracurricular, or other nonacademic activities. The same program options and nonacademic services that are available to students without disabilities must be available to students with disabilities. Program options typically include art, music, industrial arts, clubs, home economics, sports, field trips, and vocational education. Nonacademic services and extracurricular activities typically include athletics, health services, recreational activities, and special interest groups or clubs.

## Justification for Placement

The IEP must include an explanation of the extent, if any, to which the student will not participate with students without disabilities in the general education curriculum and regular classroom, as well as in extracurricular and other nonacademic activities. A justification for placement must be provided on the IEP.

# What Are Assistive Technology Devices and Services?

As part of developing a student's IEP, the IEP team will consider the student's need for assistive technology devices and services.

Assistive technology devices are defined as any item, piece of equipment, or product system that is used to increase, maintain, or improve the functional capabilities of a student with a disability. Assistive technology devices can be acquired commercially off the shelf, modified, or customized. Since the explosion of technology in our country, assistive technology devices have become more widely available and have been shown to dramatically improve the functional capabilities of a student with a disability in mobility, communication, employment, and learning. Many of the devices have been instrumental in allowing students with disabilities to be educated in regular classrooms, working and learning alongside their nondisabled peers. Some examples of assistive devices are electronic communication aids, devices that enlarge printed words on a computer screen, devices that facilitate communication for individuals with hearing impairments, prosthetic devices, Braille writers, and keyboards adapted for fist or foot use.

Assistive technology services are any services that directly assist a student with a disability to select, acquire, or use an assistive technology device. This includes evaluating the needs of the student, including a functional evaluation in the student's customary environment. The term also includes such services as

- Purchasing, leasing, or otherwise providing for the acquisition of assistive technology devices by students with disabilities
- Selecting, designing, fitting, customizing, adapting, applying, maintaining, repairing, or replacing assistive technology devices
- Coordinating and using other therapies, interventions, or services with assistive technology devices such as those associated with existing educational and rehabilitation plans and programs
- Providing training and technical assistance for the student with a disability or, if appropriate, the student's family
- Providing training and technical assistance for professionals (including individuals providing education or rehabilitation services), employers, or others who provide services to, employ, or are otherwise substantially involved in the major life functions of that student

# What Are Related Services?

In general, related services are defined as transportation and such developmental, corrective, and other supportive services as are required to assist a student with a disability to benefit from special education. The following are included within the definition of related services:

- Speech-language pathology and audiology services
- Psychological services
- Physical and occupational therapy
- Recreation, including therapeutic recreation
- Early identification and assessment of disabilities in students
- Counseling services, including rehabilitation counseling
- Orientation and mobility services
- Medical services for diagnostic or evaluation purposes
- School health services
- Social work services in schools
- Parent and guardian counseling and training
- Transportation

It is important to recognize that not every student with a disability will require all the available types of related services. As under prior law, the list of related services is not exhaustive and may include other developmental, corrective, or supportive services (such as artistic and cultural programs, art, music, and dance therapy) if they are required to assist a student with a disability to benefit from special education in order for the student to receive FAPE.

As states respond to the requirements of federal law, many have legislated their own related service requirements, which may include services beyond those specified in IDEA. Further, if it is determined that a student with a disability requires a particular supportive service in order to receive FAPE, that service can be considered a related service and must be provided at no cost to the parent or guardian.

School districts may not charge parents and guardians of eligible students with disabilities for the costs of related services that have been included on the student's IEP. Just as special and general education must be provided to an eligible student with a disability at no cost to the parent or guardian, so, too, must related services when the IEP team has determined that such services are required in order for the student to receive FAPE and have included them in the student's IEP.

## How Is a Student's Placement Determined?

In some states, the IEP team serves as the group making the placement decision. In other states, the decision may be made by another group of people. *In all cases, a parent or guardian has the right to be a member of the group that decides the educational placement of the student.*

Placement decisions must be made according to IDEA's least restrictive environment requirements—commonly known as LRE. These requirements state that, to the maximum extent appropriate, students with disabilities must be educated with students who do not have disabilities.

The law also clearly states that special classes, separate schools, or other removal of students with disabilities from the general educational environment may occur only if the nature or severity of the student's disability is such that education in regular classes with the use of supplementary aids and services cannot be achieved satisfactorily.

The needs of the student will determine whether his or her IEP may be carried out in the regular class (with supplementary aids and services, as needed), in a special class (where every student in the class is receiving special education services for some or all of the day), in a special school, at home, in a hospital and institution, or in another setting. A school system may meet its obligation to ensure that the student has an appropriate placement available by

- Providing an appropriate program for the student on its own
- Contracting with another agency to provide an appropriate program
- Utilizing some other mechanism or arrangement that is consistent with IDEA for providing or paying for an appropriate program for the student

The law requires that the public agency ensure that a continuum of alternative placements is available to meet the needs of students with disabilities for special education and related services. This continuum must include instruction in regular classes, special classes, special schools, home instruction, and instruction in hospitals and institutions, and make provision for supplementary services (such as resource room or itinerant instruction) to be provided in conjunction with regular class placement.

## What Happens After the IEP Is Written?

When the IEP has been written, parents or guardians must receive a copy at no cost to themselves. IDEA also stresses that everyone who will be involved in implementing the IEP must have access to the document. This includes the student's

- General education teacher(s)
- Special education teacher(s)
- Related service provider(s) (for example, speech therapist)

- Any other service provider (such as a paraprofessional) who will be responsible for a part of the student's education

Each of these individuals needs to know what his or her specific responsibilities are for carrying out the student's IEP. This includes the specific accommodations, modifications, and supports that the student must receive, according to the IEP.

## How Can Parents and Guardians Be Involved After Their Child's IEP Is Developed?

It is in the best interests of everyone—the parents or guardians, the public agency, and the student with a disability—that the school and the parents or guardians maintain a good working relationship. The following are some suggestions that you can make to parents and guardians to develop and maintain a positive working relationship with the professionals who work with their child:

- Let your child's teacher(s) and therapists know that you are interested in playing an active role in your child's education. Plan and schedule times to talk with the professionals working with your child and, if possible, visit the classroom or program.
- Offer to explain any special equipment, medication, or medical problem your child has.
- Ask that samples of your child's work be sent home. If you have questions, make an appointment with your child's teacher(s) or therapists to discuss new strategies to meet your child's goals.
- Ask for suggestions of how you can continue, expand, and reinforce your child's educational activities at home.
- Volunteer to be a classroom or program parent. In this way, you can observe how things work in your child's program or school and how your child interacts with others.
- Let the school or program know that you may be consulted.
- Remember that both you and the school or program in which your child is enrolled want the best for your child. Working together can make this happen.

## How Does the IEP Get Implemented?

Once the IEP is written, it is time to carry it out—in other words, to provide the student with the special education and related services in the IEP. This includes all supplementary aids and services and program modifications that the IEP team has identified as necessary for the student to advance appropriately toward his or her IEP goals, to be involved in and progress in the general curriculum, and participate in other school activities. While it is beyond the scope of this guide to discuss in detail the many issues involved in implementing a student's IEP, certain suggestions can be offered.

- Every individual involved in providing services to the student should know and understand his or her responsibilities for carrying out the IEP. This will help ensure that the student receives the services that have been planned, including the specific modifications and accommodations the IEP team has identified as necessary.
- Teamwork plays an important part in carrying out the IEP. Many professionals are likely to be involved in providing services and supports to the student. Sharing expertise and insights can help make everyone's job a lot easier and can certainly improve results for students with disabilities. Schools can encourage teamwork by giving teachers, support staff, and paraprofessionals time to plan or work together on such matters as adapting the general curriculum to address the student's unique needs. Teachers, support staff, and others providing services for students with disabilities may request training and staff development.
- Communication between home and school is also important. Parents and guardians can share information about what is happening at home and build upon what the student is learning at school. If the student is having difficulty at school, parents and guardians may be able to offer insight or help the school explore possible reasons as well as possible solutions.
- It is helpful to have someone in charge of coordinating and monitoring the services the student receives. In addition to special education, the student may be receiving any number of related services. Many people may be involved in delivering those services. Having a person in charge of overseeing that services are being delivered as planned can help ensure that the IEP is being carried out appropriately.
- The regular progress reports that the law requires will help parents and guardians and schools monitor the student's progress toward his or her annual goals. It is important to know when the student is not making the progress expected—or when he or she has progressed much faster than expected. Together, parents or guardians and school personnel can then address the student's needs as those needs become evident.

# How Often Will a Student's IEP Be Reviewed and Revised?

The IEP team must review the student's IEP at least once a year. One purpose of the review is to see whether the student is achieving his or her annual goals. The team must revise the student's IEP, if necessary, to address (for a few examples)

- The student's progress or lack of expected progress toward the annual goals and in the general curriculum
- Information gathered through any reevaluation of the student
- Information about the student that the parents or guardians share
- Information about the student that the school shares (for example, insights from the teacher based on his or her observation of the student or the student's classwork)
- The student's anticipated needs

Although the IDEA requires this IEP review at least once a year, in fact the team may review and revise the IEP more often. Either the parents or guardians or the school can ask to hold an IEP meeting to revise the student's IEP. For example, the student may not be making progress toward his or her IEP goals, and the teacher or the parent or guardian may become concerned. On the other hand, the student may have met most of or all the goals in the IEP and new ones need to be written. In either case, the IEP team would meet to revise the IEP.

# What Are Some Guiding Principles for IEP Development?

The following guiding principles for IEP development are important to ensure that each student's IEP is developed and implemented in the true spirit and intent of the law:

- The IEP development process is a student-centered process. No other issues, agenda, or purposes should interfere.
- Information provided by parents and guardians on their child's strengths and needs is a vital part of the evaluation and is critical in developing an IEP that will lead to student success.
- The input of each individual on the committee should be encouraged and valued.

- All members of the committee share the responsibility to contribute meaningfully in the development of a student's IEP.
- Meaningful efforts must be made to ensure parents and guardians and students participate in the IEP development process. Information is shared in language a parent or guardian and a student can understand.
- Special education is a service, not a place. The IEP development process evolves to address concerns and considerations so as to support the student's progress toward the state's learning standards and to ensure that the student receives services in the least restrictive environment appropriate for the student.
- The IEP recommendations are based on the student's present levels of performance and in consideration of the student's strengths, needs, interests, and preferences and the concerns of the parent or guardian for the education of their child.
- The IEP needs to be developed in such a way that it is a useful document that guides instruction and provides a tool to measure progress.
- The IEP must appropriately address all the student's individual needs without regard to the current availability of needed services.
- Positive behavioral supports and services needed by the student should be identified.
- A student's need for transition services should be considered throughout the IEP development process, as, for example, during discussions of the student's present levels of performance, projected outcomes for adult living, goals and objectives or benchmarks, services, accommodations, program modifications, and placement.
- The student's parents or guardians participate in developing, reviewing, and revising the IEP, having concerns and information considered and being regularly informed of their child's progress.
- The IEP development process should include steps to ensure IEP implementation.

## Summary of the Steps to Developing and Implementing an IEP

The IEP needs to be developed in a particular sequence, in accordance with a parent's or guardian's due process rights (for example, in giving prior notice of meetings or other actions and providing for consent and participation). The information considered and discussed in each step provides the basis for the next step in the process.

## Step 1: Obtain and Consider Evaluation Information

Evaluation information must be obtained in all areas of the student's disability or suspected disability. Evaluations need to identify and provide instructionally relevant information on the individual needs of the student, current functioning, cognitive, physical, developmental, and behavioral factors that affect learning and how the disability affects the student's participation and progress in the general education curriculum and in general education classes (or, for preschool students with disabilities, participation in appropriate activities).

## Step 2: Identify the Student's Present Level of Educational Performance

The student's present skills, strengths, and individual needs must be discussed and documented. This includes how the student's disability affects participation and progress in the general education curriculum (or for preschool students, participation in appropriate activities), consideration of specific student needs, and the student's needs as they relate to transition from school to adult activities.

## Step 3: Identify the Projected Outcomes When Schooling Is Completed

When the student reaches age 15, the committee must begin, in consideration of the student's needs, preferences, and interests, to identify appropriate outcomes for the student's projected employment, postsecondary education, and community living.

## Step 4: Set Realistic and Measurable Goals for the Student

The measurable annual goals that the student can realistically reach in the year in which the IEP will be in effect and that will move the student toward the projected outcomes at the end of schooling must be discussed and documented on the IEP. For each annual goal, measurable intermediate steps between the student's present levels of performance and the annual goals (that is, the short-term instructional objectives or benchmarks) must be identified. These goals should relate to the student's individual needs and promote the student's participation and progress in the general education curriculum in the least restrictive environment. In determining goals, the committee must discuss and document how the student's progress toward the goals will be measured and communicated to the student's parents or guardians.

## Step 5: Determine the Special Education Services the Student Will Need

The committee must consider the student's needs and goals in deciding what services and programs, as well as accommodations, program modifications, and supports the student needs.

## Step 6: Determine the Coordinated Set of Transition Activities

When the student reaches age 14, the committee must begin to identify courses of study to meet a student's transition needs; when the student reaches age 15, the committee must begin to identify the transition activities that will be provided to help the student reach his or her annual goals and projected outcomes at the end of schooling.

## Step 7: Determine Where the Services Will Be Provided

The committee must decide where the special education services will be provided. The location of services and the recommended placement must be based upon least restrictive environment requirements. Unless the student's IEP requires some other arrangement, the student with a disability must be educated in the school he or she would have attended if the student did not have a disability.

## Step 8: Implementation

There may be no delay in implementing a student's IEP, including any case in which the payment source for providing or paying for special education services for the student is being determined. The student's IEP needs to be implemented as soon as possible after the committee meeting and must be implemented as recommended by the committee.

The school must take steps to ensure that a student's IEP is implemented as recommended by the committee. A partial list of such steps follows:

- Providing copies of the student's IEP, as appropriate
- Informing each individual of his or her IEP implementation responsibilities

- Providing a student with instructional materials in an alternative format if recommended on the student's IEP

## Step 9: Measure Progress Throughout the Year

A process needs to be identified to measure the student's progress toward meeting the annual goals and report the progress to the student's parents or guardians in the format and time schedule as agreed upon in the student's IEP.

## Step 10: Review and, If Appropriate, Revise the IEP

The committee must reconvene to review the student's IEP when requested by the student's teacher or parent or guardian, but at least annually. Discussions at the IEP review meeting must consider the student's progress toward meeting the annual goals, any concerns of the parent or guardian, any new evaluation information, the student's progress in the general education curriculum (or, for preschool students, participation in appropriate activities), and the student's need for test accommodations. It must also identify the least restrictive environment for the student. For students 15 years old and older, the projected outcomes at the end of schooling should be reviewed annually.

Upon consideration of these factors, the IEP should be revised, as appropriate, to address any lack of expected progress toward the annual goals and in the general education curriculum; the results of any reevaluation and any information about the student provided to, or by, the parents or guardians; the student's anticipated needs; and any other relevant matters, including a student's need for test accommodations.

## Step 11: Conduct a Meeting to Review
## Reevaluation Information on the Student

The needs of students change over time. Therefore, a reevaluation of the student's individual needs and the continued appropriateness of the special education services that have been provided to the student must be conducted at least every three years, but more often if conditions warrant or if a parent or guardian or the teacher requests a reevaluation of the student. The committee must convene a meeting to discuss and, if appropriate, revise the student's IEP in consideration of the results of the reevaluation.

# 7

# Step VII

## Annual Review

## What Is the Annual Review?

Each year the IEP Committee is required to review the student's existing IEP and present program. During this process, the Eligibility Committee will make recommendations upon review of records that will continue, change, revise, or end the student's special education program. From these findings, the Eligibility Committee will make adjustments to the IEP and recommendations to the board of education. Further, a student's IEP must be reviewed, and revised if necessary, at least annually and more often if needed.

## When Does the Annual Review Occur?

The annual review occurs within a year of initial placement and yearly thereafter. The date of the annual review should be noted on the student's IEP. An Eligibility Committee review may be requested by the parent or guardian, the student's teacher, or a school administrator at any time to determine whether a change or modification is needed. If such a review occurs before the scheduled annual review, the next review must be conducted within one year. The annual review meeting can occur at any time during the school year, but many districts choose to review the IEP in the spring. The annual review meeting must occur by June 30.

## How Is a Parent or Guardian Notified of the Meeting?

Parents and guardians will be notified by mail of the date, time, location, and individuals expected to attend the student's meeting. The parent or guardian will also be given a statement about his or her right to bring other people to the meeting. While the date may vary from district to district, parents and guardians should play a proactive role in this process and call the committee if they have any questions.

## What Takes Place at an Annual Review Meeting?

At the annual review meeting, the team reviews the student's progress toward the IEP goals and the benchmarks of the general education curriculum. They will consider the results of any reevaluations, information about the student, including information provided by the parents or guardians, classroom-based assessments, and the observations of teachers and related service providers. They will also discuss the student's anticipated needs for the coming year and other relevant matters.

At the annual review meeting, the team revises goals and objectives (including the introduction of new goals and objectives) and determines the student's program, including placement and the need for supports and services.

The next year's IEP is developed from the discussion at the meeting. The annual review meeting may consist of more than one session to effectively develop a new IEP.

## What Rights Are Afforded to the Parent or Guardian Under Due Process During the Annual Review?

As earlier stated, the parents and guardians have the same rights that they had at the initial Eligibility Committee meeting. The parents or guardians will also be notified that if they cannot attend the meeting, they will have the opportunity to participate in other ways such as through telephone calls or written reports of the annual review meeting. If necessary, they will be able to have an interpreter provided at no cost to them. The student's notice of the annual review will include the right to have information about the planned review. A parent or guardian may at any time inspect the student's school files, records, and reports and make copies at a reasonable cost. Such records can be very helpful at the meeting. If medication or a physical condition is part of the student's disability, parents or guardians may request that a physician attend the meeting. A parent or guardian may request an independent evaluation or an impartial hearing or appeal the decision to the state review office of the state education department.

A parent or guardian is also entitled to receive free or low-cost legal services and a listing of where those services can be obtained. Parents and guardians are also entitled to pendency, that is, leaving the student in the current educational placement during the formal due process proceedings, unless both parties agree otherwise. Parents and guardians may be able to obtain reimbursement for attorney's fees in special education disputes in which they prevail.

After the annual review, parents and guardians will receive another notice about the recommendation that has been made to the board of education. A copy of the student's IEP will be sent to parents or guardians if the student has been recommended to continue to receive special education. The notice will also explain all factors used to make the recommendation. Again, the notice will describe a parent's or guardian's due process rights.

## Who Participates in the Annual Review?

The participants at the annual review meeting include the parent or guardian, the student (if appropriate), at least one general education teacher (if the student is now or may be participating in the regular classroom), at least one special education teacher or special education provider, at least one student study team member who can interpret instructional implications of evaluation results, the case manager, a representative of the school district (who has the authority to make decisions), and, at the discretion of the parent or guardian or the school district, other individuals who have knowledge of the student or special expertise relevant to the educational and other IEP decisions, including related services personnel as appropriate.

Whenever transition services are to be considered or discussed, the student must be invited to the meeting, along with a representative of any other agency that is likely to be responsible for providing or paying for transition services.

Further participants at the annual review may be the school psychologist, the guidance counselor at the secondary level, a medical doctor if the case involves medical issues, an interpreter (if required), and anyone the parent or guardian wishes to bring as an advocate.

## Is a New IEP Developed at the Annual Review?

Yes. One of the major goals of the Eligibility Committee at the annual review is to develop the new IEP for the coming school year. This does not necessarily mean that major changes are made each year, but rather any necessary changes that might provide greater or more realistic support and intervention for the student. The parent or guardian should be encouraged to play a very active role in the development of this new IEP, since it can have a profound effect on his or her child's experience in special education.

The areas that parents and guardians will most want to get involved with (**refer to Step VI: IEP Development**) will be annual goals and objectives, related services, accommodations and modifications, transition services if the student is of age, participation in general education, and parent or guardian feedback concerning progress.

## What Might the Parents and Guardians Be Asked at the Annual Review?

While the issues may vary from meeting to meeting and district to district, for the most part the parent or guardian may be asked the following:

- Have you seen progress this year in academic areas? If not, what have you noticed?
- Have you seen progress in social areas? If not, what have you noticed?
- Do you feel that the student benefited from his or her related services?
- Do you feel that the student benefited from the accommodations and medications provided?

- Do you feel that the committee should consider additional related services or modifications and accommodations? If so, which ones and why?
- Are you aware of and did you receive a copy of the student's triennial evaluation results? (asked in a triennial review year)
- Do you have any further questions about the triennial evaluation results? (asked in a triennial review year)
- Do you feel the student benefited from his or her special education placement?
- Would you suggest a change in that placement? If so, for what reasons?
- Do you have any concerns about his or her current classification? If so, what are the concerns and what would you suggest?
- Has your child been evaluated outside the school this year in any manner: medically, educationally, psychologically? Would you like to share those results with the committee?
- In a year where transition services are in effect, parents and guardians should ask about the transition plans for the year. The committee may ask the parents or guardians if they have any feelings about the work experience or postsecondary education they would like to see for their child after he or she ages out.
- What goals would you like to see for your child in the coming year?

# What Happens If the Parent or Guardian Disagrees With the Recommendations Made at the Annual Review?

The parent or guardian should be very vocal at the annual review meeting and allow the committee the opportunity to find a suitable resolution if a disagreement arises. In many cases, any differences can be resolved at that time. If differences cannot be resolved to the satisfaction of the parent or guardian, then, as with any meeting of the Eligibility Committee, the parent or guardian will receive notice of the committee's recommendations in the mail along with a copy of the proposed IEP for the coming year. At that point, the parent or guardian may appeal the recommendations made by the committee by writing a letter to the board of education indicating disagreement with some or all of the recommendations made at the annual review. (**Refer to Step V: Procedural Safeguards Under IDEA.**)

## What Suggestions Should Be Made for the Parent's or Guardian's Participation in the Annual Review?

- Suggest ways to meet their child's proposed goals and objectives as specified in the IEP.
- Discuss changes or additions for their child's upcoming program and services. Talk about what worked and what needs adjustment from their point of view.
- Ensure that the IEP that was developed at the Eligibility Committee meeting in order to determine the effectiveness of the program throughout the year, and make parents or guardians aware of the areas where the student showed success and significant progress.
- Discuss high school diploma and credential options.
- Discuss any need for a referral to an adult service provider, that is, the state **vocational rehabilitation** coordinator, for services the student may need as an adult.
- Review problems that they or their child have experienced or encountered throughout the year with the IEP Committee and staff.
- Ask questions about their child's proposed goals in the IEP and request whatever additional information they need.
- By age 13, the parent or guardian should begin to consider plans for occupational education and transition services.

## What Record-Keeping Ideas Should Be Suggested to the Parents and Guardians During the Annual Review?

Parents and guardians should be encouraged at the start of each year to save copies of the most current IEP, report cards, samples of their child's work, and teacher conference reports. They should also save copies of all notices from and correspondence with the IEP Committee during the year. Last, they should save a copy of their child's IEP developed at the annual review meeting.

# 8

# Step VIII

## The Triennial Evaluation

## What Is the Triennial Evaluation?

Under IDEA 2004, a student must be reevaluated at least every three years. This is known as a triennial review. The purpose of the triennial review is to find out

- Whether the student continues to be a "student with a disability" as defined within the law
- The student's current educational needs

The reevaluation is similar to the initial evaluation. It begins by looking at the information already available about the student. More information is collected only if it is needed. If the group decides that additional assessments are needed, the parents or guardians must give their informed written permission before the school system may collect that information. The school system may go ahead without their informed written permission only if they have tried to get the parents' or guardians' permission and they did not respond.

Although the law requires that students with disabilities be reevaluated at least every three years, the student may be reevaluated more often if a parent or guardian or a teacher requests it.

*(a) General. A public agency must ensure that a reevaluation of each student with a disability is conducted in accordance with Secs. 300.304 through 300.311—*

*(1) If the public agency determines that the educational or related services needs, including improved academic achievement and functional performance, of the student warrant a reevaluation; or*

*(2) If the student's parent/guardian or teacher requests a reevaluation.*

*(b) Limitation. A reevaluation conducted under paragraph (a) of this section—*

*(1) May occur not more than once a year, unless the parent/guardian and the public agency agree otherwise; and*

*(2) Must occur at least once every 3 years, unless the parent/guardian and the public agency agree that a reevaluation is unnecessary. (Authority: 20 U.S.C. 1414(a)(2))*

## What Professionals Are Involved in the Triennial Evaluation?

Who composes the team that will reevaluate the student will depend on the information already obtained, the age of the student, and state guidelines. For instance, if a student has had several intelligence tests over the years, the IEP Committee may not require a new one if the results have been consistent from test to test. Therefore, the psychologist may not be involved at this meeting. It is best for parents to ask the chairperson of the IEP Committee or a member of the assessment team which professionals will be doing the assessment and what areas they will be evaluating; that is, the special education teacher may be evaluating reading, math, spelling, and writing levels along with processing ability.

## How Will the Parents or Guardians Find Out About the Results of the Triennial Evaluation?

Once the triennial evaluation is complete and the report generated, parents or guardians should hear from a member of the assessment team who will set up a meeting to go over the results. In some districts, this may occur before the annual review, and in others, it may occur at the annual review if it is also a triennial year. Parents or guardians should ask the team members when they will be hearing about the results when they are brought in for an update of information from the last testing. They may also contact the chairperson of the IEP Committee and ask when they should expect to hear the results of the triennial evaluation.

## What Information Will the Parents or Guardians Be Asked to Provide During the Triennial Evaluation?

In most cases the parents or guardians will be asked to update any information since the last triennial evaluation or since the initial evaluation if this is the first triennial. This update might bring up the following questions, among others:

- What has changed in the family situation: that is, health issues, new jobs, loss of jobs, new house, death, new births, and so on?
- What has changed at home in the student's peer interactions?
- What has the student's emotional state been since the last evaluation: that is, any increase or decrease in tantrums, reactions, compliance, depression, calmness, or other emotional manifestations?
- What has been the parents' or guardians' perception of progress in school since the last evaluation?
- Have there been any outside evaluations done on the student since the last evaluation: that is, medical, psychological, and educational?
- Have there been any major changes in the student's health or medical status since the last evaluation?
- Have there been any traumatic experiences since the last evaluation?
- Have there been any changes in sleep or eating habits since the last evaluation?
- Is the student on any medications? If so, for what conditions?
- Has the student sustained any falls or injuries since the last evaluation?
- Has the student participated in any sports activities, groups, or organizations since the last evaluation? If so, what have the student's experiences been with these activities?
- Has the student exhibited any changes in physical ability, coordination, or muscle control since the last evaluation?

## What Suggestions Should You Make to Parents and Guardians About Their Participation in the Triennial Evaluation?

Parents and guardians should be encouraged to check records at home and make sure an evaluation is scheduled every three years. When parents are notified of the triennial evaluation, they may want to request additional evaluations that may provide them with a more comprehensive assessment of the student's needs. If parents or guardians have questions about new tests, they should call the IEP Committee for information. A parent or guardian should be encouraged to ask about the type of assessment instruments that will be used, the purpose, what they measure, and how results will be reported: that is, objectively, like grade equivalents or percentiles, or subjectively, like a general analysis. Before the meeting, parents and guardians should ask to review evaluative results and write down any questions they may have regarding reports.

## What Record-Keeping Ideas Should Be Suggested to Parents and Guardians During the Triennial Evaluation Phase?

Parents and guardians should be encouraged to try to record the names of tests that are given each year and keep an ongoing record of test results from the triennial evaluation. It will be important that they keep a copy of every triennial evaluation. They are entitled to have a copies of these evaluations, and if they do not receive them, they should make a request in writing to either the chairperson of the IEP Committee of someone on the assessment team.

# 9

# Step IX

## Transitional Services From School Age to Adult Life

## What Are Transitional Services?

Transitional services are a coordinated set of activities monitored by the school that are designed to prepare the student for positive experiences in adult life. According to IDEA 2004, Sec. 300.42, transition services:

*(a) Transition services means a coordinated set of activities for a student with a disability that—*

*(1) Is designed to be within a results-oriented process, that is focused on improving the academic and functional achievement of the student with a disability to facilitate the student's movement from school to post-school activities, including postsecondary education, vocational education, integrated employment (including supported employment), continuing and adult education, adult services, independent living, or community participation;*

*(2) Is based on the individual student's needs, taking into account the student's strengths, preferences and interests; and includes—*

*(i) Instruction;*
*(ii) Related services;*
*(iii) Community experiences;*
*(iv) The development of employment and other post-school adult living objectives; and*

*(Continued)*

(Continued)

> *(v) If appropriate, acquisition of daily living skills and functional vocational evaluation.*
>
> *(b) Transition services for students with disabilities may be special education, if provided as specially designed instruction, or a related service, if required to assist a student with a disability to benefit from special education.* (Authority: 20 U.S.C. 1401(34))

## Who Is Entitled to Transition Services?

As part of the student's Transitional IEP, secondary education students with disabilities, ages 15 through 21, are eligible to receive transition services. The transitional process could be initiated earlier for students younger than 15 who are considered to be at risk of dropping out of school. Cultural and linguistic backgrounds of disabled students must be taken into consideration when delivering transitional services. While guidelines are provided in federal legislation, there may be some variation in the start of transitional services in some states.

## What Areas Are Included Under Transitional Services?

### Occupational or Vocational Education

Participation in occupational education programs can provide important experiences and specific vocational training.

### Postsecondary or Continuing Education

Starting in junior high school, the student's IEP should include educational goals that prepare him or her for further education or vocational training.

### Legal/Advocacy

Advocacy is speaking up for oneself and working with others to make systems work for one. People with disabilities have the right to an opportunity for working, living, and socializing in the community.

### Transportation and Travel Training

The ability to use transportation options is crucial for independence. Inability to use transportation, or the lack of accessible transportation, can seriously limit social and work opportunities.

## Financial/Income

Planning in advance is the best way to avoid difficulty at a later time. The school district may be able to provide information on how to get assistance in financial planning.

## Personal Independence/Residential

Independence is about self-determination. An individual with disabilities can be independent while living with family or friends. He or she may even choose to live alone and have support staff to provide assistance.

## Medical/Health

Maintaining good health allows one to focus on life activities and goals that have been set. Specific areas are medication, ongoing medical care, fitness and nutrition, insurance, Medicaid/Medicare, management of personal assistance.

## Employment

It is important for one to consider all the work experience options when selecting a career, such as competitive employment, enclave, job coach, supported employment, **sheltered workshops,** employer support, and volunteering.

## Recreation/Leisure

Everyone needs a break from work and school. Having fun is an important way to get mental and physical exercise. It is also a good way to meet people and to make new friends. Specific areas are community recreation activities, leisure activities, special interest areas, hobbies.

## Assistive Technology

The Individuals with Disabilities Education Act (IDEA), the federal special education law, provides the following legal definition of an assistive technology device: "any item, piece of equipment, or product system . . . that is used to increase, maintain, or improve functional capabilities of individuals with disabilities" (20 U.S.C. Chapter 33, Section 1401(25)).

## Social and Sexual Issues

Today, because of the work of advocates and people with disabilities over the past half-century, American society is acknowledging that those with disabilities have the same rights as other citizens to contribute to and benefit from our society. This includes the right to education, employment, self-determination, and independence. We are also coming to recognize, albeit more slowly, that persons with disabilities have the right to experience and fulfill an important aspect of their individuality, namely, their social life and sexuality.

## Self-Determination

What it means and how to help the student develop self-determination is the topic of this section. One of the most significant concepts to emerge in the last few decades is the awareness of the importance of self-determination in the life of an individual with a disability. For too long, professionals made decisions for people with disabilities with little input from the individual or parents and guardians. While these decisions were motivated by good intentions, they may have overlooked the desires, hopes, and aspirations that remained hidden within the person with disabilities. As our society has become more sensitive to the needs and rights of people with disabilities, we have come to recognize self-determination as a crucial element in a life plan.

# What Is the District's Role in Transition Services?

Districts are required to develop a strategic plan for incorporating transition services within the IEP process and will need to implement transition planning and services. The Eligibility Committee will need to identify outcomes for the student to reach when schooling ends and will need to include activities in the transitional IEP that prepares the student for participation in the adult community.

The intent of the transition process provided by the district is to enable the student with a disability to live, work, and continue to learn in the community with supports if necessary as adults. The process of developing transition plans involves the following:

- Active student participation
- Active family members' participation
- Active community service agencies' participation
- Active school district personnel participation

A documented, sequential transitional process should include services that are provided for students from linguistically and culturally diverse backgrounds, a focused plan that is measured in terms of what the student is able to successfully achieve in the transition to adult life, and timely support and services that are agreed upon in the Individualized Transition Education Program (ITEP) by the parent or guardian and his or her child.

## What Is an Individualized Transitional Education Program (ITEP)?

The TEP or ITEP is that part of a student's IEP that deals with transition service goals and experiences. The ITEP should include long-term adult outcomes from which annual goals and objectives are defined. Transition services should prepare the student to pursue his or her desired long-term adult goals through a variety of activities:

- Instruction
- Community experiences
- Development of employment
- Adult living objectives when schooling is completed
- Activities of daily living
- Functional vocational evaluation

The following should be addressed in the ITEP:

- A statement of transition services that is responsive to the student's preferences, interests, and needs (The beginning date for the service should be provided.)
- Annual goals and objectives that include the following ten areas:
  1. Education; that is, college
  2. Legal/advocacy; that is, guardianship
  3. Independence/residential; that is, private residence versus **group home**
  4. Recreation/leisure; that is, joining sports activities
  5. Financial/income; that is, banking and checking accounts
  6. Medical/health; that is, health insurance and physician selection
  7. Employment; that is, sheltered workshop versus competitive employment
  8. Transportation; that is, public versus private
  9. Postsecondary or continuing education; that is, college versus vocational training
  10. Other support needs such as clergy or fraternal organizations

- Long-term adult outcomes in the IEP, including statements on the student's performance in employment, postsecondary education, and community living

- A coordinated set of activities that must demonstrate the use of various strategies, including community experiences, adult living objectives, and instruction (If one of these activities is not included in the IEP in a particular year, then the IEP must explain why that activity is not reflected in any part of the student's program. Activities of daily living and functional vocational evaluation activities should also be included.)
- A list of participants involved in the planning and development of the ITEP

Under existing regulations, the committee on special education must notify the parent or guardian when an initial evaluation, review, or reevaluation is being conducted.

## What Should the Student and Family Participation Be in the Transition Process?

Below are steps that the family can take to assist in the transitional process:

- Explore their community for useful community resources
- Discuss transition options with other families
- Provide peer support to other parents and guardians
- Seek out information about occupational, educational, and living options
- Work along with the school to find ways to increase their child's academic, career, and personal independence skills
- Set achievable goals for their child
- Help their child develop the ability to communicate needs, preferences, and interests to school staff and other professionals
- Observe the kinds of things their child can do independently and the areas in which he or she may need assistance
- Participate actively in meetings with the school and other professionals
- Make sure they plan and prepare well in advance for their child's future financial, medical, and housing resource needs, as appropriate, by assisting with an application for Social Security Disability or Supplemental Security Income (SSI) benefits, developing a will, determining guardianship, applying for financial aid for postsecondary education or training
- Help their child obtain key identification documents, as a Social Security card, driver's license, or nondriver identification card
- Help their child develop independent decision-making and communication skills

- Help their child explore options and set realistic goals for the future.
- Enhance their child's positive self-esteem and assist him or her to develop independence, including self-reliance, self-advocacy, and self-management skills
- Use actual home-life opportunities to teach their student daily living skills, such as banking, shopping, cooking, cleaning, and laundry
- Promote good money management, budgeting, and savings
- Encourage their child to become aware of the world of work, such as by talking with neighbors
- Helping their child to locate and obtain a part-time job
- Reinforce work-related behaviors at home (grooming, etiquette, following directions, completing chores, and the like)
- Provide opportunities for leisure time activities; that is, sports, daily exercise, or hobbies
- Encourage their child to participate in social activities with peers
- Teach their child how to utilize community resources (library, recreation, transportation, stores, and so on)
- Work actively with their Eligibility Committee to make sure the plan is successful
- Stay in close contact with their child's teachers

## What Is a Vocational Assessment?

A vocational assessment is the responsibility of the district's special education committee. Professionals who are a part of this committee begin by assessing referrals for special education services and continue throughout subsequent annual reviews. The planning of transitional services includes the IEP Committee's development of transitional employment goals and objectives based on the student's needs, preferences, and interests. These will be identified through the student-centered vocational assessment process.

A good vocational assessment should include the collection and analysis of information about the student's vocational aptitudes, skills, expressed interests, and occupational exploration history (volunteer experiences, part-time or summer employment, club activities). The collection of this information should also take into account the student's language, culture, and family.

A Level I vocational assessment is administered at the beginning of the student's transitional process and is based on the student's abilities, expressed interests, and needs. The Level I assessment may include the review of existing school information and the conduct of informal interviews. A Level II vocational assessment usually includes the administration of one or more formal vocational evaluations. A Level III vocational assessment usually involves the analysis of the student's success in a real or simulated work setting. The analysis is usually reported by a job coach, employer, or vocational evaluator. The transitional process should not be used to limit the student's educational or career aspirations. Instead, it allows districts to provide opportunities at an earlier age.

The Level I takes a look at the student from a vocational perspective. A trained vocational evaluator or knowledgeable special education teacher should be designated to collect the Level I assessment data. The information gathered for analyses should include existing information from

- Cumulative records
- Student interviews
- Parent or guardian and teacher interviews
- Special education eligibility data
- A review of the student's aptitudes, achievements, interests, behaviors, and occupational exploration activities

The informal student interview involved in a Level I assessment should consider the student's vocational interest, interpersonal relationship skills, and adaptive behavior.

A Level II assessment follows and is based upon the analyses obtained from the Level I assessment. A Level II assessment may be recommended by the IEP Committee at any time to determine the level of a student's vocational skills, aptitudes, and interests but not before the age of 12. The same knowledgeable staff members involved in prior assessments should be used. Data should be collected on the student's

- Writing
- Learning styles
- Interest inventory
- Motor abilities (dexterity, speed, tool use, strength, coordination)
- Spatial discrimination
- Verbal comprehension in reading
- Perception (visual, auditory, and tactile)
- Speaking and communicating facility
- Numerical fluency (measurement, money skills)
- Comprehension (in task learning and problem solving, for example)
- Attention (staying on task)

A Level III vocational assessment is a comprehensive vocational evaluation that focuses on real or simulated work experiences. This assessment is the basis for vocational counseling. Unlike a Level I or Level II assessment, a trained vocational evaluator should administer or supervise a Level III assessment. Options include

- Vocational evaluations, including aptitudes and interests, which are compared to job performance to predict vocational success in specific areas (Work samples must be valid and reliable.)
- Situational vocational assessments, which occur in real work settings (This on-the-job assessment considers what has been learned and how.)
- Work performance assessments, which are progress reports from supervisors or mentors that provide information on the student's job performance (A standard observational checklist may be utilized.)

If the student plans a postsecondary educational program, he or she may benefit from two types of assessments:

1. General assessments of postsecondary education skills are necessary to determine the student's academic skills, critical thinking skills, requirements for reasonable accommodations, social behaviors, interpersonal skills, self-advocacy and self-determination skills, learning strategies, and time management or organizational skills. This information is usually obtained in consultation with peers or teachers or in a self-evaluation.

2. Assessments specific to the field of study or setting are necessary to assess the student's needs in relation to daily living skills that may be experienced in a classroom setting or on a college campus. The parent or guardian may need to identify additional skills that his or her student must plan for to be an effective member of a postsecondary educational setting such as
   - Dormitory living versus commuting
   - Lab work
   - Large lecture versus seminar courses

The parent or guardian may wish to visit campuses that provide support services for students with disabilities. Sources of information on colleges that provide support services can be obtained in a local library or bookstore.

In order to involve the expertise of community nonschool personnel in the transitional planning process, the issue of confidentiality must be addressed. Under the Family Education Rights and

Privacy Act (FERPA), known as the Buckley Amendment, the parent's or guardian's rights to confidentiality must be maintained. The parent or guardian may need to sign releases to provide written consent during the transition process to benefit from the resources in the community. The parent's signature does not commit the parent or guardian or the student to a specific service if the parent or guardian later feels he or she does not want or need them. Have the parent or guardian ask the district about the rules of confidentiality for the release of information, the use of information by community agencies, and the storage of information by the district.

## What Concerns Should Parents and Guardians Be Aware of If Their Child Will Be Entering a Work Situation After Aging Out?

The student in an employment situation after aging out will be making a transition with difficult barriers. Two specific problems currently facing students are that those who serve them may lack effective, community-based transition programs from school to work and, second, not have the cumulative combined experience of a time-tested coordinated service. There is no process that enables education, rehabilitation, and business professionals in local communities to have effective services to meet the needs of these youths and employers who will help them coordinate the process of transition.

In the workplace, students with disabilities may have further problems. Beyond high school they have problems learning new skills and are less able to adapt to change. They may exhibit difficulties with interpersonal relationships in the workplace as well as difficulties in work habits, initiative, and reliability—skills necessary in the workforce. Employers today need self-sufficient people who can think for themselves, people who can show initiative. Is the student a self-starter who can fend for himself or herself, or is he or she dependent on others to complete a task?

## What Are the Different Types of Work Situations Available to Students With Disabilities?

When speaking to students about work situations you can inform them of the following:

## Option I: Competitive Employment

This road to employment involves competing with other people to get and keep a job. Job competition may sound scary, but it is how most people get their jobs, including the family and service providers. Being employed competitively means that you are working in a regular work setting, alongside coworkers who aren't mental health clients, and you're working for an hourly wage, usually at or just above minimum wage.

Doing it on one's own means that one conduct the job search alone using newspaper want ads, asking people one knows if there are openings where they work, or looking for help wanted signs at local businesses. One handles problems at the job on one's own or by discussing the problems later with friends, family, or service providers. The manager judges how good a job a worker is doing and tells the worker what he or she is doing right and doing wrong. Both the worker and the boss decide how long the worker remains at the job.

## Option II: Supported Employment

This road to employment also involves getting competitive employment (a job that is open to any applicant). But one does not do it entirely on one's own. Supported employment helps individuals with any type or degree of disability to look for, get, and keep a job. A service provider (also called an employment specialist or placement specialist) helps an applicant decide what he or she would like to do and then helps the applicant find that job. If the applicant needs special training or support, the service provider provides it after the applicant gets the job (sometimes the employer does this instead). The job otherwise is a competitive job, as described above.

The applicant works in places and positions that match his or her preferences and abilities.

Supported employment will help an applicant every step of the way in deciding what to do, how to deal with any problems encountered, and whether to tell the boss and coworkers about unobvious disabilities. The applicant also receives help deciding how to coordinate working with receiving Social Security disability benefits. This is especially important if the intention is to work while continuing to receive full benefits. Also, with supported employment, the assistance has no time limit. The help will remain available after having been on the job for a while, or while looking for a better job while still holding the old one.

## Option III: Transitional Employment

On this road, the applicant gets the assistance of an employment specialist and works in a real job setting for minimum wage or just above. But the job is temporary. It is called a transitional placement, and it belongs to the service delivery agency. The duration of the job is usually six months, and is followed by another transitional placement or perhaps to competitive employment. There are usually fewer choices about the kinds of work in transitional placements, since they are designed to give experience, not to be a permanent job.

## Option IV: Sheltered Employment

Sheltered employment is a very different road, and one that should be taken with caution. On this road, the workers all have disabilities and the job pays less than minimum wage. Often, you do a small part of a larger job, called piecework, and the pay depends on how much work is finished, not according to an hourly wage.

Most sheltered workshops are run by social service agencies, and little or no assistance is offered to help a worker get a better job after having done sheltered work. On the other hand, the staff inside the workshop offers plenty of help whenever a worker has difficulty. Most people don't make much money in a sheltered workshop, so their benefits are not affected. Still, sheltered workshops are not the only way to work and keep the benefits. SSI and SSDI checks are often unaffected with supported employment as well.

# What Should a Parent or Guardian or Student With a Disability Consider With Postsecondary Education?

- What are admission requirements?
- What is the student's grade point average? ACT or SAT scores?
- Are there special accommodations for the student to take entrance exams?
- Are there special incentive programs?
- Is there a disabled student service office on campus?
- What kind of documentation is required to verify disabilities?
- Is there a disabled student organization on campus? How to contact them?
- How are the faculty informed of the necessary accommodations if needed?
- Is tutoring available? Is it individual or group? Is there a cost?
- Are note takers and readers available? Is there a cost? How are they trained?

- Is it possible to arrange for tape recorder classes, computers, untimed testing, test readers?
- Is it possible to relocate classes to more accessible sites?
- What is the college's policy on course substitutes or waivers of curriculum requirements?

The parent or guardian will need to work closely with the child to prepare him or her for postsecondary education. It is important that the parent or guardian investigate several college programs to find a good fit for the child.

When the student is accepted into a postsecondary school, in order to become successful, the student needs to assume the responsibility to communicate his or her needs to friends, to instructors, and to the clerical and clinical staff in the school.

Following are some basic clues to relationships with instructors and professors.

- They are a key part of the education.
- They are paid to teach.
- Like the student, they will expect to be treated with respect.
- Instructors expect students to be adults.
- Students need to ask for help when they need it.
- Students must accept responsibility for mistakes they make.
- Professors aren't likely to be tricked. It doesn't work; sooner or later a student will get caught.
- A student should make up his or her own mind about a teacher. Some instructors are good for some students but not for others.
- A student should get to know the instructor firsthand and talk to him or her. Instructors are also human. Sometimes they look intimidating, but a book can't be judged by its cover. The instructor may be a nice person who wants to help students succeed.
- Arriving early for class is a good habit. It gives time for relaxing and speaking to the instructor or classmates or just sitting and reviewing notes.
- Being ready with paper, pencils, and any reading materials needed for that particular class is essential. Being prepared gives a good feeling and shows commitment.
- Sitting in the front of the class would be a good idea, close to the professor and to the blackboard. Sitting at a distance from the front of the room may create a tendency to daydream.
- Remaining focused can be hard, but if keeping on doing it becomes easier and so will learning the materials and the textbook to bring success in life.

- Asking questions and participating in class are good, but not if it interrupts the lesson. The time for questions is when the professor stops. Raising one's hand shows courtesy. Also, if the professor seems unclear, he or she can be asked to repeat something or explain. If it is the lesson that is unclear, a student should speak to the professor after class. This way the professor gets to know the student and can feel the student's interest in the class.
- Criticism from the professor is another way of learning, it is not a personal insult. It is the teacher's job to correct students.
- Classwork should be submitted as one would to an employer.
- Having to revise work should not be a source of discouragement. Accepting revision willingly shows a serious attempt to learn.
- For problems with a particular subject or more complete answers in privacy, the best rule is to set up a meeting and keep the appointment. Being early or at least on time is common courtesy. If a meeting must be canceled, it should be done as early as possible and only if there is no choice.
- The best way to make an appointment is to leave a phone message or a note taped to the professor's office door. The note should give the teacher an idea of what the meeting is about. That way, the teacher will probably have the answer to most of the questions. Instructors are real people and are there to help.

Here are the most common questions a student should ask himself or herself at this time:

- Why do you want to go to college?
- How do your parents or guardians feel about you going to college?
- What would you like to major in?
- What is your learning disability? How does it affect you?
- What are your weaknesses?
- What things are easy for you to learn?
- What things are difficult for you to learn?
- What helped you learn in the past?
- What help do you need from our program to make it in college?
- Will you spend extra time and effort to be successful in college?

# Glossary

**Ability grouping.** The grouping of students based on their achievement in an area of study.

**Accelerated learning.** An educational process that allows students to progress through the curriculum at a faster pace.

**Achievement.** The level of a student's accomplishment on a test of knowledge or skill.

**Adaptive behavior.** The collection of conceptual, social, and practical skills that people have learned so they can function in their everyday lives.

**Adaptive physical education.** A modified program of instruction implemented to meet the needs of special students.

**Advocate.** An individual, either a parent or professional, who attempts to establish or improve services for exceptional students.

**Age norms.** Standards based on the average performance of individuals according to age groups.

**Agnosia.** A student's inability to recognize objects and their meaning, usually resulting from damage to the brain.

**Amplification device.** Any device that increases the volume of sound.

**Anecdotal record.** A procedure for recording and analyzing observations of a student's behavior; an objective, narrative description.

**Annual goals.** Yearly activities or achievements to be completed or attained by students with disabilities that are documented in individualized education programs (IEPs).

**Aphasia.** An acquired language disorder involving severe impairments in both comprehension and production.

**Articulation.** The production of distinct language sounds by the speech organs.

**At risk.** Having a high potential for experiencing future medical or learning problems.

**Attention deficit/hyperactivity disorder (ADHD).** A psychiatric condition characterized by poor attention, distractibility, impulsivity, and hyperactivity.

**Baseline measure.** The level or frequency of behavior prior to the implementation of an instructional procedure that will later be evaluated.

**Behavior modification.** The techniques used to change behavior by applying principles of reinforcement learning.

**Bilingualism.** The ability to speak two languages.

**Career education.** Instruction that focuses on the application of skills and content area information necessary to cope with the problems of daily life, independent living, and vocational areas of interest.

**Categorical resource room.** An auxiliary pull-out program that offers supportive services to exceptional students with the same disability.

**Cognition.** The mental process of knowing, including aspects such as awareness, perception, reasoning, and judgment.

**Consultant teacher.** A support specialist for students with disabilities who provides the services in the classroom.

**Criterion-referenced tests.** Tests in which the student is evaluated on his or her own performance according to a set of criteria and not in comparison to others.

**Declassification.** The process in which a student with a disability is no longer considered to be in need of special education services. This requires a meeting of the Eligibility Committee and can be requested by the parent or guardian, by the school, or by the student who has passed the age of 18.

**Deficit.** A level of performance that is less than expected for a student.

**Desensitization.** A technique used in reinforcement learning in which there is a weakening of a response, usually an emotional response.

**Diagnosis.** The specific disorder(s) identified as a result of some evaluation.

**Distractibility.** Difficulty in maintaining attention.

**Due process.** The legal steps and processes outlined in educational law that protect the rights of students with disabilities.

**Dyscalculia.** A serious learning disability in which the student has an inability to calculate, apply, solve, or identify mathematical functions.

**Dysfluency.** Difficulty in the production of fluent speech (e.g., stuttering).

**Dysgraphia.** A serious learning disability in which the student has an inability or loss of ability to write.

**Dyslexia.** A severe type of learning disability in which a student's ability to read is greatly impaired.

**Dysorthographia.** The learning disability associated with spelling.

**Enrichment.** Provision of a student with extra and more sophisticated learning experiences than those normally presented in the curriculum.

**Etiology.** The cause of a problem.

**Exceptional student.** Any child who requires special instruction or related services.

**Free appropriate public education (FAPE).** Special education and related services that are provided at public expense and conform to the state requirements and to the individual's IEP.

**Group home.** A residential living arrangement in which several adults with disabilities, especially those who are mentally retarded, reside with several supervisors without disabilities.

**Habilitation.** An educational approach used with exceptional students that is directed toward the development of the necessary skills required for successful adulthood.

**Homebound instruction.** A special education service in which teaching is provided by a specially trained instructor to students who are unable to attend school. A parent or guardian must always be present at the time of instruction. In some cases, the instruction may take place on a neutral site and not in the home or school.

**Hyperactivity.** Behavior that is characterized by excessive motor activity or restlessness.

**Impulsivity.** Non-goal-oriented activity exhibited by individuals who lack careful thought and reflection prior to a behavior.

**Inclusion.** Returning students with disabilities to their home school so that they may be educated in the same classroom with students who are not disabled.

**Individualized education program (IEP).** A written educational program that outlines the current levels of performance, related services, educational goals, and modifications for a student with a disability. This plan is developed by a team including the student's parent(s), teacher(s), and support staff.

**Interdisciplinary team.** The collective efforts of individuals from a variety of disciplines in assessing the needs of a student.

**Intervention.** Preventive, remedial, compensatory, or survival services made on behalf of an individual with a disability.

**Itinerant teacher.** A teacher hired by a school district to help in the education of a student with a disability. The teacher is employed by an outside agency and may be responsible for several students in several districts.

**Learning disability.** A disorder in one or more of the basic psychological processes involved in understanding or in using spoken or written language, which may manifest itself in an imperfect ability to listen, think, speak, read, write, spell, or do mathematical calculations.

**Least restrictive environment (LRE).** An educational setting for exceptional students and students with disabilities that minimizes their exclusion from students without disabilities.

**Mainstreaming.** The practice of educating exceptional students in the general classroom.

**Mental age.** The average level of intellectual functioning for students of a given chronological age. When dealing with students with severe disabilities, the mental age may be more reflective of levels of ability than the chronological age.

**Mental disability.** A disability in which the individual's intellectual level is measured within the subaverage range and there are marked impairments in social competence.

**Native language.** The primary language used by an individual.

**Noncategorical resource room.** A resource room in a general education setting that provides services to students with several types of disabilities. The students with these disabilities are able to be maintained in a general school setting.

**Norm-referenced tests.** Tests that compare a student's performance to the performance of others on the same measure.

**Occupational therapist.** A professional who programs and/or delivers instructional activities and materials to help children and adults with disabilities participate in useful daily activities.

**Paraprofessionals.** A trained assistant who helps a classroom teacher provide instruction.

**Physical therapist.** A professional trained to assist individuals with disabilities and to help them maintain and develop muscular and orthopedic capability and make correct and useful movements.

**PINS (person in need of supervision) petition.** An appeal to a family court from the school or the parent to seek remedies for a student under the age of 16 who is out of control in attendance, behavior, or some socially inappropriate or destructive pattern.

**Positive reinforcement.** Any stimulus or event that occurs after a behavior has been exhibited that increases the possibility of that behavior occurring in the future.

**Pupil personnel team.** A group of professionals from the same school who meet at regular intervals to discuss students' problems and offer suggestions or directions for resolution.

**Pupils with special educational needs (PSEN).** Students defined as having mathematics and reading achievement lower than the 23rd percentile and requiring remediation. These students are not considered to have disabilities but are entitled to assistance to elevate their academic levels.

**Related services.** Services provided to students with disabilities to enhance their ability to learn and function in the least restrictive environment. Such services may include in-school counseling and speech and language services.

**Remediation.** An educational program designed to teach students to overcome some deficit or disability through education and training.

**Resource room.** An auxiliary service provided to students with disabilities for part of the school day. It is intended to service students' special needs so that they can be maintained within the least restrictive educational setting.

**Response to intervention (RTI).** A three-tiered model established under IDEA 2004 as an alternative to the discrepancy model for determining whether a student has a learning disability.

**Screening.** The process of examining groups of students to identify at-risk students.

**Section 504.** Part of the Rehabilitation Act of 1973 in which guarantees are provided for the civil rights of children and adults with disabilities. It also applies to the provision of services for students whose disabilities are not severe enough to warrant classification but could benefit from supportive services and classroom modifications.

**Self-contained class.** A special classroom for exceptional students, usually located within a general school building.

**Sheltered workshops.** A transitional or long-term work environment for individuals with disabilities who cannot, or who are preparing for, work in a regular setting. Within this setting the individual can learn to perform meaningful, productive tasks and receive payment.

**Surrogate parent.** A person other than the student's natural parent who has legal responsibility for the student's care and welfare.

**Token economy.** A system of reinforcing various behaviors through the delivery of tokens. These tokens can take the form of stars, points, candy, chips, and so on.

**Total communication.** The approach to the education of students who are deaf that combines oral speech, sign language, and finger spelling.

**Underachievement.** A discrepancy between a student's actual academic achievement and expected academic achievement. It is important that the school identify the underlying causes of such underachievement because it may be a symptom of a more serious problem.

**Vocational rehabilitation.** A program designed to help adults with disabilities obtain and hold jobs.

# References and Suggested Readings

American Speech-Language-Hearing Association. (2005). *Speech-language disorders and the speech-language pathologist.* Retrieved September 10, 2005, from http://www.asha.org/students/professions/overview/sld.htm

Bureau of Labor Statistics, U.S. Department of Labor. (2004–2005). Teachers—Special education. *Occupational outlook handbook.* Retrieved November 28, 2005, from http://www.bls.gov/oco/ocos070.htm

Chandler, J. (2004). *What is a learning disorder?* Retrieved September 10, 2005, from http://www.klis.com/chandler

Department for Learning and Educational Achievement. (2006). *Student study teams: Mission statement.* Golden, CO: Jeffco Public Schools.

Deutsch-Smith, D. (2004). *Introduction to special education: Teaching in an age of opportunity* (5th ed.). Boston: Allyn & Bacon.

Friend, M. (2005). *Special education: Contemporary perspectives for school professionals.* Boston: Allyn & Bacon.

Friend, M., & Bursuck, W. D. (2002). *Including students with special needs: A practical guide for classroom teachers* (3rd ed.). Boston: Allyn & Bacon.

Fuchs, L. S., & Fuchs, D. (2001). Principles for sustaining research-based practice in the schools: A case study. *Focus on Exceptional Children, 33*(6), 1–14.

Fuchs, L. S., Fuchs, D., & Speece, D. L. (2002). Treatment validity as a unifying construct for identifying learning disabilities. *Learning Disability Quarterly, 25,* 33–45.

Gargiulo, R. M. (2004). *Special education in contemporary society: An introduction to exceptionality.* Belmont, CA: Thompson-Wadsworth.

Giler, J. Z. (2000). *Socially ADDept™: A manual for parents of children with ADHD and/or learning disabilities.* CES Continuing Education Seminars. Retrieved September 13, 2005, from http://www.ldonline.org/article.php?max=20&id=770&loc=47

Grandin, T. (2001, June). *Teaching tips for children and adults with autism.* Retrieved February 19, 2002, from http://www.autism.org/temple/tips.html

Groves, M. (2001, June 14). The nation: Routine autism screening should be done at an early age. *Los Angeles Times*, pp. A1, A4. Retrieved March 12, 2002, from Academic Universe/Lexis-Nexis database.

Hardman, M. L., Drew, C. J., & Egan, M. W. (2005). *Human exceptionality: School, community, and family.* Boston: Allyn & Bacon.

Heward, W. L. (2006). *Exceptional children: An introduction to special education* (8th ed.). Upper Saddle River, NJ: Pearson Education.

Individuals with Disabilities Education Improvement Act. (2004). Pub. L. No. 108-446, 118 Stat. 2467 (2004).

LDOnline. (2005). *Learning disabilities.* Retrieved September 10, 2005, from http://www.LDOnline.org

Lerner, J. W. (2003). *Learning disabilities: Theories, diagnosis, and teaching strategies* (9th ed.). Boston: Houghton Mifflin.

Marcus, L. (2002, January 10). *Inclusion for children with autism: The TEACCH position.* Retrieved February 19, 2002, from http://www.teacch.com/inclus.htm

Mesibov, G. (2002, January 10). *Learning styles of students with autism.* Retrieved February 19, 2002, from http://www.teacch.com/ed

Mestel, R. (2001, March 12). Special report: Autism. *Los Angeles Times*, p. S1. Retrieved March 12, 2002, from Academic Universe/Lexis-Nexis database.

National Joint Committee on Learning Disabilities. (2005). *Responsiveness to intervention and learning disabilities.* Washington, DC: Author. Retrieved September 12, 2006, from http://www.ldonline.org/about/partners/njcld

Office of Vocational and Educational Services for Individuals with Disabilities. (2002). *New York State Department of Special Education in New York State for Children: Ages 3–21 (a parent's guide).* Albany: State University of New York.

Olson, J. L., & Platt, J. M. (2000). *Teaching children and adolescents with special needs.* Upper Saddle River, NJ: Prentice Hall.

Palmer, A. (2002, January 10). *Strategies for surviving middle school with an included child with autism.* Retrieved February 19, 2002, from http://www.teacch.com/survmidd.htm

Pierangelo, R., & Giuliani, G. (2006a). *Assessment in special education: A practical approach* (2nd ed.). Boston: Allyn & Bacon.

Pierangelo, R., & Giuliani, G. (2006b). *Learning disabilities: A practical approach to foundations, assessment, diagnosis, and teaching.* Boston: Allyn & Bacon.

Thurlow, M. (2005). State policies on assessment participation and accommodations of students with disabilities. *Journal of Special Education, 28*(4), 232–235.

Turnbull, R., Turnbull, A., Shank, M., & Smith, S. J. (2004). *Exceptional lives: Special education in today's schools* (4th ed.). Upper Saddle River, NJ: Prentice Hall.

U.S. Department of Education. (2004). *Twenty-sixth annual report to Congress on the implementation of IDEA.* Washington, DC: Author.

Young, S. (2005). *No child left behind: History.* Retrieved September 12, 2006, from www.ncsi.org/programs/educ/NCLBhistory.htm

# Index

**CORWIN PRESS**

The Corwin Press logo—a raven striding across an open book—represents the union of courage and learning. Corwin Press is committed to improving education for all learners by publishing books and other professional development resources for those serving the field of PreK–12 education. By providing practical, hands-on materials, Corwin Press continues to carry out the promise of its motto: **"Helping Educators Do Their Work Better."**